Please Find Herein

Stampfel On Weber

No One You'd Care to Meet

Antonia, my partner/lover 1962/1978, told me a number of stories about a notorious speed freak named Steve Weber, who she used to sort of go out with. She said he went around barefoot in New York City for eight months and never cut his feet or stepped in dogshit. He taught her about country blues by playing her records that had details he wanted to show her. He would play the record over and over until she got it, never mentioning just what the "it" he wanted her to get from that particular record was. But she always knew, and always eventually got it. She would never say when this happened, but he would always know and not play it again.

She eventually wrote a number of songs about him. This one is called "Sentimental Song":

I used to have a friend, no one you'd care to meet
Sometimes I'd pretend I could keep him off the street
I have a peaceful life ahead of me
Though he had funny ways, we knew each other's tastes
We would fight for days. It took up all the space
I have a peaceful life ahead of me
Now I have no more friend. We just ran out of luck
Would I do it again? Not for a million bucks
I have a peaceful life ahead of me

And this one is called "I Disremember Quite Well":
You'll pardon me if I look strange, but we've been out of touch
I know that time is on your side, but time can do so much
Are you still making it with time?
I disremember
Quite well
I can see as I look close time has been good to you
Just for a moment's truth you almost had the face I knew
But now, of course, it's not the same
I disremember
Quite well
I used to know you when you changed your water into wine
You played the shell game with yourself and won it every time
But where are you going to keep your prize?
I disremember
Quite well
I used to walk on water too, and float above the sand
And pour the stars like diamonds through my outstretched
greedy hands
But I've forgotten how that game goes
I disremember
Quite well
And did you ever do whatever thing it is you're for
Or does an old idea like that have meaning anymore?
The maybe that I loved has gone, but where?
I disremember
Quite well

I had pictured this Weber guy as scary and grizzled and older
than me, although Antonia eventually told me he was the handsom-
est man she had ever met. Ed Sanders said, in a copy of his time-
less periodical, *Fuck You: A Magazine Of The Arts*, that Weber had
recently had an all-night sexual romp with a gazelle in the Central
Park Zoo. To this day I'm very gullible and used to be even more so.
I thought, "Wow, that's really cool", assuming the gazelle was up for
an all-night-long hook up, and with critter rape, under the circum-

stances, being unlikely. But no, Weber never did that. I don't think there was even a gazelle in the zoo.

In any event, I was surprised when he showed up at our apartment in May. He was actually 19 years old, about six-foot four, and resembled an idealized Lil' Abner. *Lil' Abner* was a comic strip than ran from 1934 to 1977, but most people alive probably don't have a mental picture of him. Some people consider it the greatest comic strip in history. Daisy Mae, who finally married Lil' Abner in 1952, was the archetype upon which Dolly Parton built her image. (Please go to Google if no images come to mind and broaden your cultural horizons.)

My instant feeling was that here was the long lost brother I never knew I had. The first thing my long lost brother and I did was snort some crystal meth and play music. I didn't expect him to play country blues, much less to do it so well, with a degree of syncopation I never heard in another finger-picker until I heard Joseph Spence later that year. (Again, if you're unfamiliar, go to YouTube and check Spence out. Try "Out On The Rolling Sea When Jesus Speaks To Me".)

Right away we sounded like we'd been playing together for years, and we found we had learned dozens of songs from the same sources. Also our voices worked great together. We kept on playing for hours. When evening came it was time for me to go to work at my gig in the basket-passing coffee house in the Village. Naturally, I invited Weber along, and our first public performances ensued. Public response was instantly enthusiastic. We played several sets and went back home to continue playing. This went on for three days: snort crank (which was not called that yet; he shot up, I never did), play all night and day, gig in the evening, repeat.

On the third evening we were playing at the Café Raffio, where there was a mirror against the back wall to stage right where performers could see how they looked on stage. I glanced at the mirror, and was thunderstruck by our mutual appearance: long hair for those pre-Beatle times, my droopy moustache, our old-timey vests and black boots, his killer good looks, and my not nearly-as-killer but still pretty good looks. In general terms, our appearance was a combination of dangerous and goofy, definitely something brand-new. This was back when folk singers mainly looked what they used to call "clean-cut". Good lord, I thought, we're one of the most amazing things I've ever seen in my life. This must not stop! But our three-day idyll was about to come to an end. We were playing the Café Flamenco across the street, both of us on stage sitting on chairs, when I suddenly hit a bad note. Weber winced as though he had been shot, and on the next beat, he hit a bad chord, which he followed, also right on the beat, with four increasingly worse chords. Upon hitting the last one, he screamed and leapt from the stage and ran towards the door, guitar in hand. I instantly gave myself a shove so I started falling backwards, chair and me hitting the floor just as he hit the door. I knew intuitively I would hit the floor just as he went out the door. Man, we were synched up. In the space of six beats we went from playing along smoothly to him running down Bleecker Street and me being flat on my back on the stage floor. Wow, I thought, this is GREAT! There's no way we can stop!

I was soon to find out that after Weber was up for three days he tended to get an attack of the anti-socials and light out for the territory, as it were. But I was determined that our musical relationship would become permanent.

What I didn't know was that this had been Antonia's plan all along. She felt the two of us had much to learn from each other, and that we should pursue a professional career together. Also, it was her plan to get Weber off the street. But part of her plan was to rig it so we'd think it was our idea, a typical feminine ploy, and completely successful.

At first, Weber didn't want to acknowledge this. When I said time to go to work, he's say, "No! No! It's evening, so we might as well go to the Village. And since we're going to the Village, we might as well take our instruments along..."

But we needed a name. So we tried Flotsam Warp and Jetsam Woof. Fast Lightning Kumquat and Wild Blue Yonder. Orville Swamp Bucket and Prescott Dregs. The Total Quintessence Stomach Pumpers. For awhile Weber was torn between calling himself Teddy Boy Forever or Teddy Boy Always. (I preferred Teddy Boy Forever.) We decided we'd keep tossing names out there until people tossed them back.

Then we tried Total Modal Rounders. One day when we were all high on pot, my friend, Steve Close, who was once sprayed with blood when a Chicago meth monster (as some A-heads were called, no one said speed freak yet) standing in front of him shot himself up in the neck, said, "Holy Modal Rounders" and I thought, yes! Bingo! Score! Jackpot! We finally had a name.

Conventional wisdom at the time said if you were going to negotiate a record contract, you needed a manager, whose job it was to book gigs as well. There was a manager who was always around the scene named Jack Solomon. Everyone knew he was a manager because, although he was always around on the scene, he always wore a suit and tie. The three record companies we were considering were Elektra, Vanguard and Prestige. They were all interested, but we decided to go with Paul Rothchild, the A&R man for Prestige, solely because he smoked pot, and consequently smoking pot in the studio while recording would not be a problem.

However, the problem turned out to be Paul Rothchild. There was something creepy about him, like when we went into a deli on the Lower East Side, and he started eating food from the display before he paid for anything. Naturally, the guy behind the counter told him to cut it out and pay for it first. Paul proceeded to throw a fit over his will being thwarted. His attitude was that he was being a groovy free spirit-child and the clerk was being some kind of authoritarian square. Paul stomped out of the store.

Also, when it was time to sign the contract, he had us smoke a lot of pot, then "explained" the contract to us, which was to say, he lied about a number of details. Then he insisted that we should be a trio, because we played string band music, and everybody knew string bands were trios, like the New Lost City Ramblers. I asked what about Grayson and Whittier, an old time duo from the '20s, or the Blue Sky Boys, a duo from the '30s? Although he had never heard of either, he knew better.

Well, ok, we tried working with Luke Faust as a trio, but although that worked ok on some songs, it didn't on others. Besides that, Luke wasn't comfortable playing with two A-Heads. But the real problem was that a couple weeks after signing us to Prestige, he quit and went to Elektra, which would have been the best label choice by far. So there we were, stuck on a label in which we knew no one. Gee, thanks, Paul.

But the gigs were going fine. We worked in three different basket houses, going from one to the other. Strangely, every single time we got to the next club, it was exactly time to go on. Every club had about three acts, and the sets were about the same length, so it made sense. The odd part was how perfectly the time always worked out. Weber didn't want to pass the basket, but I didn't mind. I was used to it.

The only time I minded was every seventh set at the Café Raffio. It happened every seventh set and it only happened there. Each time, there would be a full house, every seat packed. But the entire audience would sit there in total silence, staring at us, but not looking at us in a zombie-like way. After each song, no one would applaud. Not a mutter or even a whisper the whole set. Then I'd have to pass the basket, putting it in front of each face, while every face refused to make eye contact. I would end up with maybe 50 or 75 cents total, never even as much as a dollar. Every seventh set and only at the Raffio.

Also weirdly, we had a strange confrontation at the Café Flamenco with two of the lowest echelon mobsters I ever heard of. They were trying to...well, I never did figure out what they were trying to do. It seemed to be about some kind of kickback, only since we were just passing a basket in one of the smallest houses in the Village, I wasn't sure what was supposed to be kicked back. A percentage of each basket collection? But we were arguing back and forth, and when it would go one way, one of the junior mobster guys would hand me a dollar bill, and when it would go the other way, he would snatch it away. The dollar bill got handed and snatched back several times. It was almost as surreal as the silent zombie crowd.

Our first out-of-town gig was in Boston, not really a gig, more of an exploration. A music store was having a marathon hoot to collect money for a children's hospital and we were invited up to perform. There was going to be a prize of a new instrument case for whoever performed for the longest accumulated time. Since Weber and I were speeding, that made us a shoe-in, and I won the case, which I really needed because mine had disintegrated while I was carrying my banjo across Washington Square Park a few weeks previously. It burst open and dumped my banjo on the ground, with no damage thankfully. By the time we set off for Boston, I was using rope to hold my case together.

The Rounders were responsible for a major breakthrough regarding drug perception in Boston. Naturally we were asking around for who had some pot, and two guys, let's call then Joe and Al, had some but wanted to make sure we didn't tell anyone about them having any. One of the guys, let's call him Joe, had his stashed in the inner lining of a billed sailor cap, a classic standby. He said be sure you don't tell Al that he smokes pot. Thing is, we had already got some pot from Al, who said be sure you don't tell Joe, etc. But the thing was, the two had been close friends for years! Of course, we told them, look, Joe and Al, you've both been smoking pot for years, and maybe it's time to retire the secret. I heard shortly after that the Boston/Cambridge crowd started to consider, you know, everyone isn't a cop, and it's ok to let some people know you smoke pot. So, who for sure isn't a cop? Hmm...the Holy Modal Rounders...

Weber had been telling everybody that he had written one of our most popular song's, "Euphoria". One of Michael Hurley's sisters (backstory: Michael Hurley, Robin Remailly and Weber had been friends since 11th grade in Bucks County, PA; strangely, they met at exactly the same time I arrived in New York from Milwaukee) told Robin that Weber was going around telling everybody that he had written "Euphoria", which had actually been written by Robin in 1962. It would not be the last time Weber attempted to take credit for a song he didn't write. Needless to say, Robin was very pissed, and headed for New York. As it happened, both Weber and I had taken some peyote a few hours before Robin's unexpected arrival. He pounded on the door, and I answered it. I had heard about Robin and Hurley from Weber, but hadn't met them yet. In comes pissed-off Robin. One of the first things about him I noticed was his shirt, a well-worn wool shirt in two tones of green. I had never seen anything like it. "What a beautiful shirt," I said. "Take it, it's yours," he said, whipping it off and handing it over, to my surprise and delight. Wow, I thought, I had never seen anyone actually give anybody the shirt off his back before. I could have hardly had a better first impression of Robin. Antonia and I retired to the west end of our apartment while Robin chewed Weber out in the east bedroom where Weber had been living since May. We politely didn't eavesdrop, although I wanted to.

We never did get invited to the Newport Folk Festival, for which we would have been a shoe-in if we had been on Elektra. While the current Festival was going on, we, on the other hand, had a gig in Atlantic City. We were walking down a street, and noticed a gaggle, a pretty big one, of over a dozen late-middle-aged women across the street carrying on a loud, exited group conversation while various members kept pointing at us. It was so strange we had to watch them for a while. When they saw us watching them, their excitement increased and they got even louder. Then they went into a group huddle, various members still sneaking glances at us. Finally, the huddle ended and came apart. Something had obviously been decided.

A spokesperson had been elected and the gaggle pushed one of the ladies forward. They all watched with continued excitement as the chosen one crossed the street towards us, a short, sweet, round faced woman, a little overweight, about fifty. She had been chosen to find out just what we were. She asked questions and we both tried to answer her in a way that would explain something. We weren't being rude or scary, obvious goodwill and honest curiosity were afoot. We tried to explain folk music, but it wasn't working. Finally, I tried, "We do hootenanny". Her eyes lit up, the veil had been lifted! She threw her arms up, not her whole arms, the parts attached to the body remained parallel to the ground while her forearms and palms went up, and she exclaimed, "Hootenanny!" Then she scampered across the street to the eagerly awaiting crowd and put her arms up in exactly the same way, exclaiming, "Hootenanny!" Then every single one of them threw their arms up in exactly the same way, and they all went "Hootenanny!" together. Then they all waved. We waved back. Fuck, that was way cooler than the Newport Folk Festival.

Our first recording session was set for what turned out to be the day before Kennedy got shot. Sam Charters was assigned to be out A&R man. That meant artist and repertoire man. Nowadays, they say, "producer". A&R referred to the fact that, back then, artists very seldom had their own material, and part of the A&R person's job was to line up songs for the artist to record. We, of course, had our material ready to go, and there wasn't much for Sam to actually do. We got together with Sam and his wife, Ann, who was a scholar. Actually, they were both scholars: Sam being one of the first scholars of country blues, and Ann, being among other things, one of the foremost authorities of Beat culture and literature.

Oddly enough, she also read palms. More oddly still, Weber and I both had an identical line on our palms she said had never seen. Still odder yet, I just looked for it, and it's mostly faded away. We explained to Sam, "Look, we smoke pot before we play", and he was ok with that. We also snorted meth, which apparently new to him, as he went around afterwards saying the Rounders sniff glue. I've never sniffed glue or any inhalants. I always found them scary.

The night before the recording, Antonia suggested we take a long walk through the city that I felt I was really going to become more of a part of. Making a record was an especially big deal then, or, at least, it sure was for me. As it was still pre-Beatles, we both got haircuts before the album cover shoot. Our hair was still long by then current standards, but our cover shot would have been cooler if it had been left its normal 1963 length.

The session went well, we cut most the album, needing just one more session to finish it. But the next day I was lying in bed and Antonia called to say the president had been shot dead. I'm ashamed to say that my first thought was, oh, no, Phil Ochs is going to write a song about it.

In late 1963, we had another gig in Boston. While there I got very sick with some kind of bad flu. I associated being so sick with my meth use (the speed kills meme was becoming established) and I knew it was, at least, not a healthy habit. I stayed with Dave Wilson, editor of *Boston Broadside*, for over a week in his spare room. The good part was it was full of old comic books. The bad part was the bed was full of crabs, which I had acquired once before. Thankfully, I never got them again. But I did quit speed. Weber and Antonia didn't, but I had no problem with that.

I was having a great year. We got a $500 advance for our album, or $250 each. Our $60 monthly rent was $40 from Antonia and I and $20 from Weber. A new Martin D-28 back then went for about $400, for further reference. Weber and I bought pony skin shoes on Delancey Street. They had actual pony hair coat in various, real pony hair colors, so you could pet them and it would feel like petting a pony. All the girls wanted to pet our shoes. That was fun. I also bought brown riding boots and a three-tone suede jacket with a V pattern in front that Antonia and I saw in a window on 8th Street and fell in love with.

Our album came out and it sounded pretty good. It's a classic, actually, and has cycled through three labels, remaining in print for over fifty years. I've asked how many copies of the damn thing has sold, and they keep telling me they don't know. What a pain in the ass.

We wanted to get out of our Prestige contract, which was for two albums, and go to Elektra. Our plan was to keep original material off the last album we were committed to and stay on the low-key, lackluster side so they wouldn't want to renew our contract. Again, Sam Charters was our man in the studio and we recorded it in two sessions. One of the songs, "Chevrolet Six", was worked out for the first time in the studio. We just ran through it three times and recorded it.

Chester Anderson wrote the liner noted this time. Prestige didn't even bother taking new photos for the cover. They just used outtakes from the first session so our hair was now out of date as well, since the Beatles had arrived after we recorded our first album.

What really pissed me off was that they didn't ask me about the sequencing, and let this total asshole do it. I do not recall said asshole's name, but he was one of those dipshit guys who had a girl-friend who was much smarter, better looking, and more competent then he was. I know that happens a lot--still does--but it used to happen a lot more. Asshole-dipshit had a practically non-stop smirk on his face as I complained, and a slow condescending way of speaking. What he managed to do was put the songs in the very worse order possible, all the songs in the same key and tempo in a row, and bad opening and closing choices. I confronted him with this. All the while I told him what he had done, he continued his non-stop smirk, followed by no apology. To this day, I regret not punching his goddamn nose.

Much worse was to come. Jack Solomon was no longer our manager, and a manager in Massachusetts had expressed an interest in taking over. However, he wasn't actually doing anything. We decided we should pay him a visit and have a talk. Our friend Jane was driving to Boston in her Volkswagen Beetle and offered to drive us up. Weber and I got in the car, but within a block it was clear that Jane was a pretty lousy driver. Weber screamed, "Stop the car!" He leapt out the door and ran. I should have followed him.

On the road, Jane explained that she had already rolled two Land Rovers. I was getting nervous, and thought maybe I should play banjo while we were riding along to help me relax. So I did, and it helped. But then a pheasant flew across the road and Jane certainly didn't want to hit the poor birdie, so instead she rolled the car over. Three for three. My window had been rolled up, but broke in the process of rolling. Seat belts were still uncommon back then. I don't know how many times the car rolled, but I was hurled out the thankfully broken window, hitting my back right below my head on my way out, landing on the side of the road.

Next thing I knew, there were two priests with stricken faces, giving me Extreme Unction, the Catholic sacrament intended for the dying. "Go away!" I yelled. "I don't want it! I quit the church!" But they kept on Unctioning me. To this day I regret not having said something more on the order telling them to go shove Holy Mother Church up their priestly asses.

The car actually came to rest on top of Jane, but she was a big woman and eventually came out of it in pretty good shape. The neck of my banjo, on the other hand, was in four pieces. My back hurt like hell. They took us to a hospital where the doctor didn't even give me an aspirin. For hours after the accident, Bob Dylan was in my head, singing "The Chimes Of Freedom". I don't remember how I got to the manager guy, who was not very sympathetic, or helpful in any way. That was our last contact.

I made it back home with my broken banjo, where the Framingham doctor continued to send me bills. He wouldn't give me a goddamn aspirin. I certainly wasn't going to give him any goddamn money. The X-rays didn't show any damage, or the hospital did a shitty job, or something, but it turned out I had a thoracic fracture which resulted in god knows how many thousands of dollars in chiropractic bills, but it could have been much worse. For starters, I could've been dead or paralyzed.

Another noteworthy event in which I did something stupid (but ultimately educational) was when we did a concert at Bard College. It took place in a large lecture hall where there was a big blackboard next to us while we played. There was also a bunch of alcohol around and it had been maybe a couple years since I got drunk on booze, so I made the classic rookie mistake of mixing hard liquor, beer, and wine. Not to mention that my tolerance was low, it had been a while, something I neglected to take into consideration. (I don't know if I started drinking while we were playing, or afterwards. Oddly, I'm about to find out, as I was just contacted by someone who recorded the concert. Possibly it will sound decent enough to release. I'm very curious to hear it.) But the stupid thing I did besides getting throw-up drunk was to, in the middle of our concert, write on the blackboard next to us, Peyote For Sale!, with instructions on where to send how much money.

How I relished the enormous gasp! that went up when I wrote it all down. My heart was in, if not the right place, a consistent place, being I was firmly in favor of ingestion of pot and hallucinogens. However, in giving direction, I neglected to write down: Hey, those white furry Q-Tip-like tufts, pick them off. They can irritate the throat. And take it with someone who has done it already, and remains straight while keeping you company.

Several months later two kids who had been there came up to me and said they sent away for the peyote, and took it, and had a scary and horrible time, and why did I tell them to do that? I said I was sorry. I felt like shit. The ultimately educational part was I stopped advocating anything stronger than pot.

That summer, Weber's friend Lotsoff came by with a monster jar of meth which lasted both Weber and Antonia and a few friends quite a while. It was a really big jar. The downside was all the A-heads pounding on our door-got any A? Got any A? I was still off it, so I never got into the jar.

Another bad thing going on was that Weber's behavior was deteriorating. His only household task was to clean out his room. Instead of doing this, he packed his accumulating garbage in tightly packed bags, which he packed tightly together until he had several square yards of trash, filling all the space in his room that wasn't bed. This went on all summer. His basic pattern was up for five days, the last two which would be away somewhere, then crash for three days, during which he would stagger out of his room, chug a quart of milk and stagger back to continue his crash. This came along with a stream of lovesick girls coming to the door wondering why Weber was ignoring them.

Weber changed after the Beatles came along. I think he realized that our chances of some level of success was greater than he had anticipated and he had a problem with that. The way it played out was that while performing he would go on about how sick he was of this song, and how sick he was of that song, and why can't we do anything new? And afterwards when I would bring up new songs to work out (working out a new song simply meant play the damn thing three times and it was good to go), he would stomp off. Then he stopped paying his share of the rent and I had to confiscate part of his money when we got paid. It was just $20 plus part of phone and utilities, but it was like pulling teeth. Finally, we asked him to move out. It took hours for us to clean his room out. Of course, there was a girl only too happy to put him up for nothing.

I stopped getting haircuts when I first heard the Beatles and by fall my hair was the longest it had ever been, although it wasn't that long compared to where men's hair would shortly be. Longley be. But throughout the nation, assholes and jerks were yelling, "Are you a boy or are you a girl?" I was getting this several times a day, every day. Sometimes the daily A's and J's were in the double digits. I tried to think of an impeccable works-every-time response to all these dolts. And finally got one, down at the sporting goods store. The hunter's duck call. Besides sounding like a duck, which is a very fine sound indeed, duck calls are made to produce a loud volume, because they have to reach the high sky where the ducks fly. For over a year I never ventured outside without my trusty duck call leather corded around my neck, soon to be joined with a goose call and another brand duck call with a robust variant sound. Now rather than dreading the inevitable next are-you-a, I looked forward to it. It stopped them in their tracks 98% of the time. The other 2% managed to, unlike the others, respond, along the lines of, "Oh, you're...a duck..."

Weber was getting ornery, but he was starting to make up some wonderful tunes, all with great and distinctive structures. Most of the time he was really interesting to have around. What I should have been doing then, I realized several decades later, is have him teach me how to play "Same Old Man", finger-picking the same notes as him. I understood, even back then, that his arrangement of that tune was a prefect template upon which to learn fingerpicking. But I had this irrational this-is-too-hard-for-me feeling about it. When I became aware of finger-picking, it felt to me like some immense mystery. All those notes coming out of hands and a guitar. And how different it sounded from all the other kinds if guitar sounds. The mystery seemed too mighty for me. Even had me actually spooked, especially when I heard Joseph Spence finger-pick. And I'd get this feeling deep inside my mind: I could do that. But then would come this much more powerful feeling: In your dreams, punk. I still have a thing about finger picking guitar. I still haven't learned how.

One of the biggest highlights of 1964 was when Weber, Antonia and I went to the New York World's Fair, and found ourselves in the Sierra Leone exhibit. In the old fair tradition, there was a brief teaser outside the exhibit intending to encourage people to come inside and see the show. "Watch the premier dancer of Sierra Leone's

troupe dance while holding a 300 pound drum!", said the announc-
er. Of course, we got our tickets. We were invited to check out the
drum, which was about four feet high, and had a wooden yoke-like
structure attached to the top. Weber, me and a number of others
checked it out. Definitely too heavy to lift, but we could tilt it on an
edge to get an idea of how heavy it was. 300 pounds sounded right.

So here comes the dancer. He looked about 50 or 60, a little
taller than average, not particularly muscular. He spread his arms
out maybe 45 degrees, hand about waist level, and starts doing this
very slow dance, making rather large circles. This goes on for a couple minutes, same slow, deliberate speed. Then he dances up to the
drum and slips his head into the hole of the yoke-like drum ap-
pendage. He leans back, lifting the drum into the air, and continues
doing the same slow dance he had been doing, only now with this
300-pound drum off the ground. This continues for two or three
minutes. Real slow all the way. Finally, he sets it back down. How
the hell? Some kind of shamanistic rhythm mojo? Mass hypnosis?
To this day I have no idea, but if someone had told me about it I
wouldn't believe them.

The only other thing I remember from the show (this was over
54 years ago) was this even older guy who played a one-string fiddle type instrument, with a western style bow. Just played by himself. My take was that beats any fiddle player I've ever heard. With
one string. The only other thing I've ever heard similar was a demo
by the guy who played violin with Bo Diddley in the '60s. A speed
freak girl friend of Weber's got the demo from who know where. It
sounded like Afro/jazz/hillbilly. Upon hearing it, I thought, that's
the sound I've been looking for. Still can't do it, but I'm still trying.

One of the coolest things about that year was hooking up with
the newly formed Fugs. Ed Sanders had this storefront on East 10th
Street that used to be a kosher butcher. He left the kosher butcher
sign on the window. It was called the Peace Eye Book Store officially,
and the Peace Eye Book Store And Scrounge Lounge unofficially. I
mentioned his *Fuck You! A Magazine Of The Art*s, which featured a
Weber poem, which I recall having just four lines, starting with, I
think, "Your bollix is a slimey slit", and the last line ends with "shit".

Its contents were mostly poetry written by local and far flung beat writers. My favorite parts of Ed's magazine, by far, were his one-page raves that each issue had. I would read that part and skip the rest. His writing remains one of my strongest influences. Besides selling all manner of underground magazines (still not called zines yet), he had amazing artifacts for sale. My favorite was a cold cream jar, half used, containing some pubic hairs, a jar he claimed Allen Ginsberg and Peter Orlovsky used for ass-fucking.

So one day Weber says, "Hey you should go to the Peace Eye and listen to Sanders and Tuli (Kupferberg). They've started a group, and they've got songs like one they're calling 'Coca-Cola Douche'". I practically ran. Besides Ed and Tuli, there was a drummer, Ken Weaver. Ed and Tuli had written dozens of songs. Neither of them played an instrument, they just sat down and wrote all these sex, drugs, and lefty politics songs, along with setting some more classic poets, like Swinburne and Whitman, to music. I listened to a couple of their songs, and instantly volunteered us two Rounders to be their back-up band. There's one of the noblest artistic endeavors, I thought, that I had ever witnessed. I must do all I can to assist its birth.

So we started rehearsing the songs at the Peace Eye. There were nominally some other members, but us five were the only ones who showed up for rehearsal. Not everything we tried got worked out. Sadly missing out was our version of the Silhouettes' "Get A Job":

Rim job, sha na na na, sha na na na na four times, then:
Lick lick lick lick lick lick lick lick
Yum yum yum yum yum rim job
Sha na na na, sha na na na na...
I'm in a state of ecstasy
I'm in a state if grace
Every time my sweetie sits upon my face.

Weaver played hand drums, but they kept getting stolen on his way to rehearsal. It happened about four times. Once he said they were stolen by two Puerto Ricans with a hammer. Rock'n Roll! But we worked real hard and had our debut at the Peace Eye Book Store. A number of luminaries showed up. Andy Warhol did a background painting for the stage. Some asshole ripped it up afterwards. It would be worth scary amounts of money today.

Harry Smith wanted to record the Fugs, and put them on Folkways, the label that had released his Anthology. He had a strange microphone setup, I didn't realize at the time that that he had been recording for about fifteen years, starting with wire recordings of Indian ceremonies in Washington state before World War Two.

For me, the highlight was when we were recording "Swinburne Stomp". Normally, the producer, who Smith definitely was, stays behind the glass, a soundproofed window, with the engineer and the recording console. But Smith raged up and down in the part of the studio where the recording was being made, tromping back and forth with a bottle of wine, which, right in the middle of the song, he hurled into the wall, making a mighty crash. Of course, you were supposed to be totally quiet if you were in the recording part of the studio. I was moved profoundly by the crashing bottle. It was like Weber leaping from the stage in the middle of the song. It was perfect. (Ed remembers it being a rum bottle.) That was my favorite Fugs recording moment.

My favorite Fugs performing moment was Ed's set-up to do a new Tuli song, a parody of "Goldfinger", called "Stinkfinger" (He loves cunt! Only cunt!). The brilliant stagecraft plan was for somebody to ring a buzzer offstage, and Ed would say, "Excuse me, there's a call." He went offstage, and said it was a call for Tuli, but that was all right, while Tuli was on the phone, we would have a secret mystery guest, the Masked Marvel, who was going to sing "Stinkfinger". Then Tuli comes back to the stage covered with the rattiest blanket on the Lower East Side. He had a flashlight inside the blanket so he can read the words he has just written. Only he can't see because he's covered with the blanket. And he doesn't know where the microphone is. He doesn't even know where the audience is, so he's facing the wrong way. And besides that fact that Tuli has one of the most unmistakable voices on the planet, you can see the Tuli body language even underneath the blanket. "He loves cunt!," the blanketed Tuli bellowed. "Only cunt!" Besides that, half the microphones weren't working, and the ones that were working were next to the people who didn't know all the words. Robin Remailly was in town, and playing backup for that show. As the curtain was coming down, he pulled down his pants and mooned the audience, neatly stopping the curtain in the middle with his bare ass. Everyone thought it was Sanders.

During the middle of the set, there was a table on stage with a book, onto which Weber had poured a pile of meth. Tuli had picked up the book, and spilled all the speed on the floor. Weber yelled at Tuli for spilling the speed. Tuli was so sorry. I think that happened two other times: speed on book on stage, Tuli picks up book, speed spills, Weber pissed, Tuli sorry.

What playing with the Fugs mostly reminded me of was playing with a bunch of the world's coolest kids in the world's greatest sandbox.

Our thesis is neatly encapsuled in the immortal ballad, "We're The Fugs":

We love grass
We love ass
We wanna hug her
We wanna bugger
We like it hot
We like pot
We scoff pills
We eat pussy
We ain't fussy
Oh, East Side
Were on the East Side
And we're the Fuuuuuuuuuuuuuugs!
We hate war
We love sex
Twos or three
Fours or fives
LSD
Dimethyl trip (tophane)
Grope for peace
Naked and ready

Poets and freaks
Oh, East Side
We're on the East Side
And we're the Fuuuuuuuuuuuuuuuuuuuuugs!

Boy, were we ever.

A New Level of Weberosity

Weber got a new place to stay, with our mutual friend John Townley. Like a lot of local freaks, John didn't have any curtains. We were over visiting once and John pointed out that there was a school across the street, and there were always a bunch of kids in the window watching the goings-on at their place. There was a sofa with its back to the window, and Weber and Antonia went to the sofa and put on a pantomime show in which they fabricated a number of sex acts, many improbable, some impossible, while leaving their clothes on, with most of their bodies hidden behind the back of the sofa. Ever-increasing numbers of slack-jawed school kids looked on. John and I alternated watching the kids and rolling on the floor, laughing.

We had a feeling someone was planning to rob our place. I had just got a new fiddle and an electric bass. Weber got a Wandre, or some similar-sounding name guitar, from Italy. So we asked a girl we had both known a short time to stay in our place while we played in Boston. Suddenly in Boston, Weber said, "Something's wrong", and he jumped on a bus to New York, where the girl, as it turned out, got high and freaked out and ran out of the apartment without closing the doors. The fiddle, bass and electric guitar were gone, but that seemed to be all. Not that we had much else to steal. Weber locked the door and got back to Boston.

Right after that we got a new roommate. Her name was Maggie and we met her at a gig. Antonia and I struck up a conversation with her because she was carrying an old 19th-century style guitar case that resembles a baby's coffin. A strange thing to bond over, but there you go. We all got on well immediately and it turned out she was looking for a place to stay, and, Weber being gone, we had a spare room. She was good company and it brought our share of the rent back down to $40.

Then one day, Michael Hurley came by for a visit and the two of them were mutually smitten. Hurley moved in with Maggie for a while. He was getting fed up with New York. He drew a picture of one his cartoon dogs, either Boone or Jocko, scratching his head, which was surrounded on top with a bunch of question marks. He was about to shake hands with his dick, which was drawn as a little Boone (or Jocko), reaching up a tiny hand to shake back. I'd have a bunch of question marks over my head too, under the circumstances.

Underneath the cartoon, it read: Reasons I hate New York:
1. Step in dog shit, spend too much money.
2. Everything constantly reminds me of Superduck (which was what he called his teenage runaway girl friend from 1962. I think she was also the inspiration for the song "Fooey Fooey" on the *Have Moicy!* Album).
3. I ready to float all away.

He taped the cartoon to a wall in the room next to ours. I sure wish I still had it. Shortly after this, they moved to Boston and got married, eventually having three children. All because of a guitar case that looked like a baby's coffin.

We had a gig in Baltimore that was pretty strange. There was a house where Weber, Antonia and I stayed. On the coffee table were several pages, presumably a song, called "World Untold And Naked". It was amazingly incoherent. It had a chorus, or refrain or something, the only part that re-occurred, which went:

There's just one hope I belong with

And if not, there's no one to blame.

There was a writing credit that read, The Bobbi Dylan Sextet. Antonia said it was a joke, a parody. I said it was dead serious. So when the guy who lived there showed up, we asked him in a neutral tone, "What was the story here?" He explained that he and five friends decided they were going to write a Bob Dylan song, and they each tried, for hours. Finally, everyone gave up and left their pages of attempts on the table. The guy said, "I went through them and picked out parts and put them together so it made sense." We didn't have the heart to tell him, boy, did it not.

But Weber was getting weird in a dangerous way. While in Baltimore, we went into a Hot Shoppe for lunch on a weekday. They were a chain, something like Howard Johnson's. The place was packed with people getting lunch. Weber proceeds to offer the very busy waitress behind the counter hashish and a hashish pipe. "See", he said. "This is hashish and here's a pipe to smoke it." "Come on, Weber, let's go", I said, pulling his arm.

Then there was a weird time in Syracuse. We were walking around the town during the day, with nothing to do, and we see stairs going up to some railroad tracks, so we go up to have a look. It was an abandoned railroad right-of-way. Some of the tracks had even been torn up. We walked till we came to a small trackside shack. It was empty and all the windows were broken. Everything up there was nothing but fragments and wreckage. I tried making a small cairn with broken stones on the cracked concrete the shack sat on. Weber started glaring at me with this strange angry expression. I didn't know if it was really there, or if I was projecting. I had never had a creeped-out, scared feeling about Weber, but I was getting one right there. As I said, it was a possible projection, but I was relieved to see a vehicle approaching us, riding down the track a couple blocks away, coming slow, which you sure had to up there. We both turned towards it and watched it come bouncing along. It was a couple of cops, wanting to know what we were doing up there, trespassing. We explained we were in town playing at the club, the name of which I don't remember. We said we didn't know we shouldn't be there, and we'd get right down. They were firm, but not nasty, and we were polite.

One of the last good gigs we had was in Detroit. I'm blanking out on this Detroit DJ guy's name, but he was one of the first after Bob Fass laid it down in the early '60s to embrace free-form radio, where all genres from classical to worldbeat could be heard. The Detroit guy used to play "Mr. Spaceman" from our first album whenever there was a successful space shot.

He played us one of the most amazing pieces of music I ever heard. It was a Pacific Ocean island tribe. I have no idea what people of what island. But the whole tribe was singing this this long, driving song that was the history of the whole tribe. It went on for maybe 10 minutes. Why didn't I think to ask for him to play it again? Why didn't I write down who and what? But that was an example of what he was playing on the radio.

The club where we played was called the Chess Mate. The guy who ran it was from Europe. I'm not sure what country. Southern Europe, I think. He went on and on about how the races got along in Detroit and what nice houses everybody lived in. This was about two years before the riots. He insisted on taking us on a ride through Detroit. He really wanted us to say, "The Black people live in such nice houses!" (Although nobody said Black yet.) So because we didn't, he did: "Look at all the nice houses the Negroes live in!"

We played on a television show in Windsor, Canada, right across the border. The video spent too much time focused on a close-up of somebody's foot tapping, but it was ok. Strangely, by today's standards, it was the only video or filming of the Rounders before we broke up that July. Long lost, of course.

For years I was sad about the fact that there were no Rounders recordings from 1965, when we were at the top of our game. But then, many years later, I came across a live reel-to-reel recording of one of our performances from the 1965 Detroit gig in my dead mother's hope chest. As it happened, Weber and I owed an album to Gene Rosenthal's Adelphi Records. That debt went back to 1977. One more thing I was sad about was that the seven-piece Rounders of 1970 to 1972 never recorded before the rest of the guys split for Portland. Again, curiously, the band was playing with the same great personnel for two years and we had been at the top of our game. We did make a Rounders album for Rounder Records before they left, *Alleged In Their Own Time*, but Rounder wanted an acoustic type album, not the full-blown electric plus horn band. They were willing to do two of Robin's songs with the whole band, like the never-recorded "Sea Green Dream", but Robin wasn't happy with the way it sounded, so another fine Robin song sinks beneath the waves, never to rise.

Speaking of never to rise, the rest of the guys were back on the east coast around 1977 for a funeral, and I tried to get Rounder to finally record the seven of us for the first time. The five years apart had rendered the seven us less tight than we had been, and the AC broke down during the week-long heat wave we had to record in, which also didn't help. Then Rounder bailed in the middle, and Gene

Rosenthal and Adelphi Records came the rescue. The stipulation was Gene wanted a just-Weber-and-me album, which brings us back to the 1965 reel-to-reel from Detroit.

There was going to be a listening party, with Gene, Weber and a bunch of people there. I had a burnt CD of the reel-to-reel, which sounded great, and had a number of tracks that had not been recorded prior to when the tape had been made. But afterwards, Weber and his girl friend, Judith, claimed they hadn't heard it and asked if they could take the CD home with them. And, like a really stupid person, I let them. Next thing I knew, Weber and Judith announced that Bernard Stollman was going to put the album out on his ESP label. I really did not want that to happen. The last time we recorded for Stollman in 1967, Weber, Sam Shepard, and I were supposed to get what I thought was an advance of $150 each. As it turned our, he stiffed Sam, who he didn't allow to be on the album cover, because Sam got a crew-cut as a reaction from the Summer Of Love bullshit. Never mind how cool a crew-cutted twenty-four year old Sam Shepard would have looked to posterity. Stollman would not tolerate an "unhip" haircut.

But years later, when I asked Stollman when we were going to get some royalties for the album, which by this time had been released in several foreign countries, he said the contract I signed said I none of us were due any royalties ever, and he also owned all the publishing, and the contract said he kept our share of the mechanical royalties, which are what songwriting royalties are called. Normally, the publisher gets half and the songwriter gets half. In other words, I robbed you fair and square. Didn't you read the contract?

I don't know how many of you have tried to read a music contract, but they tend to be written in legalize so dense I have trouble following them for more then a sentence and a half. Why didn't I take the contract to Terri Thal, who was still my manager? I plead dumbness in the first degree.

But I did not like the idea of Stollman putting it out, and talked to him about it. He said, "I'm always in charge, and, besides, finders keepers." In other words, it was Weber's turn to put out an album, with my dead mother's tape. I talked to a lawyer who said he could fight it, but it would take $5000 for starters.

The album, "Live in 1965", was released with a hideous cover. Stollman took Weber to the Oscar Brand radio show to promote it. Oscar asked where the tape had come from and Weber said, "Somebody's attic." My mom didn't have an attic. The album offered t-shirts for $20. I met a number of people who had sent the money for the t-shirt. None of them ever got one. Nor did Weber or myself ever see a single penny from the release.

Now I have somewhat of a quandary here. After Bernard Stollman died, I talked to ESP about my non-payment issues with them. What eventually happened was they granted the rights to the two albums back to me, hence this package. But there was one stipulation: I had to refrain from saying bad things about Mr. Stollman. But is describing bad things he did, as I did above, the same thing as saying bad things about him? I don't think so, but I'll see what others have to say. But I can say a number of good things about him, starting with our first contact. It was September 1966, and Antonia and I had been speeding for months, and were three months ($180) behind in our rent. Stollman called up out of the blue (I knew nothing about him) and said he was going to give me $180 because I was on the Virgin Fugs album.

Needless to say, my first impression of him was a very good one. And in the early aughties, he gave me and Weber each a couple hundred dollars. This is in keeping with what I was told by the current president of ESP when I called him about the issues I had. He said Stollman was a terrible record keeper, but tended to give out money when he had it. But then, when he, um, got hold of the "Live In 1965" tape, he leased it to, I think it was Water Records. When I called them I was told they had paid him $7000 for it. I tried to corroborate this after, but they never answered or got back to me. I think they're out of business. So, he certainly had some cash after that mini liquidity event, but, as I said, neither Weber or myself ever got a penny from any of the releases of this album, including no mechanical royalties from the songs we had written. But I won't say anything bad about Mr. Stollman personally.

Meanwhile, back in 1965, a new level of Weberosity manifested.

He had been making longer speed runs than his normal five-day ones, and after about a week up he talked nonstop, and every sentence had nothing to do with the sentence before or the one after. That was a new one of me. Sure wish I had recorded some of those.

At the same time he was hanging out with Brin. She was Luke Faust's GF, and Luke was going to California for the summer. Luke said he didn't mind if she slept with some other guy while he was gone, anyone except Steve Weber, who she made a beeline to as soon as he left. Hey, Luke asked for it. Besides this, for a week, Brin's younger brother was in town and hanging with Brin and Weber. The completely unconnected sentences went on for a few weeks. This is the time when Dave Gahr took all those Fug photos, which were used on their albums. I saw a whole bunch of photos from that series. Weber is vamping and posing away with profound abandon. He mainly looks really amazing, bare feet and all. It was the high water mark of his handsomeness.

Terri Thal, Dave van Ronk's wife, had been managing us since late '64, it was great to have that aspect of things under control. Meanwhile, I was relieved that Prestige had not taken up their option to continue our contract, so we were free to go to Paul Rothchild at Elektra.

Things were a little off between Paul and I. Elektra had been the obvious best choice for a label in the first place. They got their artists to the Newport Folk Festival. And had better graphics. I was eager to get with Elektra at last. But first Paul played me the first Love album, which I said I didn't like. Actually, I was having an earwax problem, I heard it several months after this, and it suddenly sounded great. But my reaction obviously offended him.

Then Paul told me about his Holy Modal Rounder revelation he had while on LSD. First! The single is not a 45! It's a 78! And! The LP has no grooves between the tracks! Isn't that great! I said, "Do radio stations still have 78-rpm turntables? And if there were no grooves between the tracks, how can a DJ pick out the track to play on the air?" Paul was outraged by my attitude towards his LSD revelation. Actually, Paul had this thing where he had to be cooler than me, and maybe cooler than anybody that happened to be around. And nothing, of course, is less cool than having to be cooler than someone.

Paul would have preferred something like, "Wow, those are the most happening ideas I have ever heard! You are truly an avatar of the hallucigeneration! Anything you say, boss!" Then, he went on to say, we had lost it musically and didn't sound good anymore. Actually, as far as our music went, we were at the top of our game. We'd been playing most of the songs for over two years and had a bunch of new ones, including two great Weber structures without words: "My Mind Capsized" and "Song of Courtship to Dame Fortune". Paul played a track we had submitted as an example of how we had gotten worse. The tune was "Baltimore Fire". I pointed out that it actually sounded great. But Paul implied if we weren't willing to do it his way and like it, he wasn't going to work with us. Why didn't Terri or I think of talking to Elektra about working with someone else there?

And, again, Weber was getting more difficult to work with. He didn't show up for one gig, the second one he ever missed. Actually, there was a third one back in '64. He had been talking about getting in touch with his birth father, who had divorced his mother when Steve was very young. One evening, Weber said he didn't feel well and asked if was it ok if I went to work alone. I told him, "Sure". And that was the night Weber's father showed up. I don't know if Weber knew he was coming or not. Weber's father never showed up again. Then Weber missed a fourth show. This was followed by a gig in Boston when, again, Weber didn't show. He had decided it would be fun to hitchhike to the gig from New York and got there a day late.

Between his increasing drug use and generally dangerous behavior, missing gigs, and bitching about being sick of the old songs when we were on stage, and worrying about him getting arrested, it looked like time was running out for us to be working together.

I had been worrying about Weber for months. The previous year we kept finding playing cards on the street. And once, on the same evening, we both found tarot cards. I found the Ace of Swords and he found a Knight of Swords, but his card had been cut in two. The two sides, top and bottom, were lying on the ground together. Then I threw an I Ching, asking about our prospects together. I got the 63rd hexagram. Then I threw it again and got the same hexagram.

It's called "After Completion" and signifies something coming to an end, and a new beginning. Well, that's what happened all right. Enough said here. Details about our breakup can be found in the Weber obituary.

Last Thoughts on Weber
Written for Perfect Sound Forever, Summer 2020

Judith Fredrick, or so she has alleged her name was, notified none of his friends when Steve Weber died February 7th, 2020. A friend of mine found his death notice in a West Virginia newspaper. That's how I found out Weber was dead. Since then my thoughts and feelings about him have been talking to each other. Processing, I think it's called. The basic theme has been: what *is* a Weber, exactly? Not that me, or anyone, could get that precise about what he exactly was.

One of my thoughts was that Weber was a basic human archetype, The Trickster. Weber, the low-key Loki. Weber, the con man. A more exalted example of the Trickster/Con Man was Harry Smith. When I met Weber, one of the first things that happened was he asked to borrow five dollars. Sure! I handed it over. Then, a few days later, he asked to borrow five dollars again, Um...ok! I handed it over. Soon he asked to borrow five dollars again. I said, "You already owe me $10." No handing over this time. I found that lend-me-five-dollars was his opening gambit for everyone he met, as were the subsequent requests that would follow. I never asked him the most five dollars loans he managed to get from a single person. A Mystery Lost To The Ages. I know he eventually stopped doing it. Or stopped doing it to other people in front of me. Yet more mystery.

The Trickster is an ancient archetype, but one of it's latter day forms could be found in the earliest comic strips, like the Yellow Kid, The Katzenjammer Kids, or Ignatz, the brick-throwing mouse. When Weber and I were kids in the '40s, there was a whole sub-genre of Tricksters in comic books, in which there was always a foil involved whose role was to be serially tricked. The Fox And The Crow--Fauntleroy and Crawford--were featured in animated films and comic books. The Crow wore a red derby, his only garment, and had a perpetual cigar in his beak, just like Woody Woodpecker, another Trickster, did occasionally. Woody sometimes had two cigars at once. But not The

Crow. The Crow spoke with a mid-20th-century Brooklyn accent. The Fox talked, and had the body language, of an up-tight white guy, and always wore a big blue bow tie that matched his pants. The plot was always the same. Foil gets tricked, except once in a while the trick would backfire. The Dodo And The Frog was another example. Pretty obvious who was who. The Frog--Fennimore--wore a black top hat, and nothing else except a cigarette holder with a bent, beat-up cigarette in it, which he never seemed to smoke. The Dodo--Dunbar-- was pink and cockeyed, that is, one eye was always lower that the other one. He wore a dorky hat with a girly little ribbon around the brim, a collar, and a really long necktie with big diagonal black and green stripes. Nothing else. The Dodo was dumber than The Fox, and the stories had a sort of heaven-protects-the-innocent theme, with The Frog's tricks almost always backfiring. There were numerous examples of this basic theme, like Bugs Bunny and Elmer Fudd.

I see Weber as a Loki-Coyote-Yellow Kid-Katzenjammer Kid-Ignatz-Crow-Frog amalgam. But he most closely resembled Flim-Flam Flamingo, who took perpetual advantage of the hard-working Petunia Pelican. Like Weber, Flim-Flam was very tall, while Petunia was quite short, and cute in a dumpy sort of way. Petunia had a job. He didn't, except hustling her for money. This was the basic pattern of Weber's life. He almost always lived with a woman who did the cooking, the cleaning, and usually paid the rent. He was massively irresponsible. He never learned to drive and always insisted on riding shotgun. He never filed taxes, never even helped set-up or strike down the band. He even tried to get others to carry his guitar case. After his marriage broke up, he came back east and lived with his mother until she had to go to a nursing home. He had a damaged shoulder from an Oregon car accident, and had fractured a femur in a car accident with Judith, so his need to be taken care of was absolute. Despite the fact that Judith isolated him from all his friends, she did take care of him. I'll give her that. But she also listening in to all his phone calls and watched what he did on computer. And accused me of stealing "the Rounder millions". What a concept! Clearly, she was delusional. Once, years ago, he managed to call a friend without her listening. "You've got to get me out of here!" he pleaded. Judith was Petunia's revenge.

But Weber was always lucky, which is a characteristic of pre-cartoon Tricksters. He was said to have one of the luckiest horoscopes of the 20th century. I'm ignorant on the subject. All I remember is Venus in midheaven and all the houses in motion, and every night is Saturday night in the zodiac. Once he had his hat shot off by a husband who had returned early. It had a bullet hole in it when he retrieved it. Another time Jeffrey Fredrick saw a commotion on the street. A bunch of people had gathered round something, which proved to be Weber rolling around and having convolutions. "I know what he just took," thought Jeffrey, "It's a good thing I have the antidote in my pocket." He quickly administered it. Another person might have died, but it was typical of Weber's luck that his savior was walking along at that very minute.

Weber, in his late teens, spent months walking barefoot in the Lower East Side with nary a step in dogshit or broken glass, much less a tetanus-tainted nail. He used to team up with a notorious Lower East Side character by the name of Ronnie Mau Mau, who sold pot and had a harem of five girls living with him. Once the cops raided his pad, finding no drugs, but discovering a big stash of then illegal pornography. "It's mine," said the youngest and most innocent looking girl. The angry cops left. But Ronnie was eventually busted. His girls made his bail by selling nickel bags, as five-dollar portions of pot were then called. Weber and Ronnie, ripped on speed, used to march down the street together, Weber playing guitar while Ronnie did a crazy dance, incorporating back flips. Everyone would flee. I'd kill for a film.

Many were awed by the spectacle of Weber taking all these drugs and doing all this deeply wild shit with a style and grace few had ever witnessed, let alone imagined. It seemed to be so effortless, so amazingly fun and so exciting too! Many young men attempted to emulate him. Many young men consequently died--most sooner rather than later. That's when people started calling him "the Fool Killer". I have no idea how many men and women Weber introduced to shooting up. My guess is easily over a hundred. One of them described how it went: *We sat down across from each other. He took my hand and looked deeply into my eyes with an ecstatic expression of crazy joy. He didn't look at my arm to seek a virgin vein. Just gave me the crazy stare-down as he hit a vein and jacked in the heroin. The rush was incredible.* Weber, the Robin Hood of the needle. He would have made a great phlebotomist.

In 1972, before the rest of the Rounders split for Portland, Oregon, we recorded *Alleged In Their Own Time* for the Rounder label, whose name was partially inspired by our band. A nice album BTW, although Rounder never released a CD version. They did, however, license the album to a Japanese label, who did issue a CD. Unfortunately, we were never informed of this. Or paid a single penny. Or even given a solitary copy. The people responsible for this... ummm, let's be kind and call it...oversight...were those who bought the Rounder catalog from the original Rounders: Bill Nowlin, Ken Irwin, and Marion Leighton. Bill gave me the contact information for those responsible or, as it turned out, those irresponsible. I was told they no longer had any records from an era as ancient as the early 21st century, and consequently were unable to address the issue in any way, shape or form. Or even give me a dime towards whatever the Japanese company paid to issue the album. Perhaps I should be grateful they didn't say, "Scram, kid, ya bother me," which a carny barker once actually said to me, in 1951. Anyway, Antonia and I had been taking fucktons of speed and doing music with Karen Dalton since late 1969, and she was going to do harmonies on two songs. Unlike Antonia and I, who drank speed mixed with fruit juice or soda pop, Karen insisted on shooting up, and "had" to do so before doing any music. So off she went to the bathroom to do so while the rest of us, all set up to record, waited in the studio. And waited. And waited some more. Finally, I went to see what was holding Karen up. She was having trouble hitting a vein. She asked me to bring Weber, the Miles Davis of the needle. She didn't say the Miles David part, just the Weber part. "Karen can't find a vein and she needs you," I told Weber. Off he stomped, muttering loudly about that damned Karen... they had been an on again/off again item. True to form, he hit her first try. Then Karen had brief convolutions, grabbed the bathroom sink, and pulled it completely off the wall. This seemed to settle her.

She marched back to the studio and laid down a perfect harmony. Rock'n Roll.

Years later in Portland, Weber was married for a while to a sweet and lovely woman, Essie, who died just a few weeks after he did. Betsy and I once asked her how her folks felt about her being married to Weber. They thought he was the nicest guy I ever went out with, she replied. And so handsome, too! The only detail I heard about prior boyfriends was that one of them like to fuck her in a coffin he had acquired for that specific purpose. Essie had the loveliest pale skin, and the tiniest little veins, which no doctor or nurse could ever hit. But Weber could, every time. Weber, the William Tell of the needle.

Sure, I loved him at the beginning, along with dozens of women who were constantly pounding on our door during the almost year-and-a-half he lived with us, before we tossed him out after three months of not paying his monthly $20 share of our $60 rent. When he left, his room was packed with stuffed bags of garbage that covered every square foot of the floor except for the skinny path from the door to his bed. And he had stolen all the silver-pre 1965-half dollars we had saved in out Brother Juniper (newspaper comic character) piggy bank. Another of his talents: Antonia and I always had special favorite glasses and cups. We never told anyone which, or that we even had, favorites. One by one, Weber "accidently" broke them all. Never any others. Only our secret favorites. How can you miss when you've got dead aim?

I was so deeply in love for the first year. I had found--had been blessed with--a musical dream partner that was unimaginably beyond anything I had been capable of dreaming of. As I've often said before, Antonia was behind our union. She thought we had much to learn from each other, and besides, it would keep Weber off the streets. But she didn't tell us of her plan, she figured, correctly, that once we met and played together, we'd think it was our idea.

In 1963 I thought there was going to be a Next Big Music Thing that would Change Everything. I thought it was going to be the Holy Modal Rounders. Ha ha ha. Remember, this was during what Dave Van Ronk used to call "the Great Folk Scare". I was half right, but it turned out to be the Beatles. Now, before the Beatles, Weber avoided thinking of our union as being professional. Once, as we were leaving for our nightly basket-passing fun, I said, "Off to work we go!" "No, no, no," said Weber. "Not work! We're just going to the Village 'cause it's evening! And as long as we're going, we might as well take out instruments..." But by early '64 the Beatles had Changed Everything, and Weber realized that we had a chance of some level of success. I don't know how many of you have seen *Bound To Lose*, the Holy Modal Rounder documentary, but there's this part where the road manager explains that whenever success beckons, Weber points the nose of the airplane to the ground and goes into a power dive.

Up to this point it had been all fun and joy. We even bought matching ponyskin shoes--they had real fur on them, and all the girls wanted to pet them. Sorry, animal activists. But suddenly Weber was bitching on stage about being sick and tired of all the old songs. And when I'd try to introduce a new one, he'd stomp off. Working out a new song never meant more than play it three times in a row. Here the irony is thicker than muck in a stable when the stable hands had been out sick for a week. For the last several years we played together, he refused to work out any new songs, mainly playing stuff from thirty years previous. Part of the problem was that his mind was not working as well as it used to. The only way to introduce a new song he could learn was to for it to just have two chords.

Anyway, by 1965 he was doing crazy dangerous stuff, like giving hashish to a waitress in a Hot Shoppe in Baltimore when it was packed with a lunch crowd. Like, staying up for a week straight, talking nonstop with never a sentence having anything to do with the sentence prior or the one following. Sure wish I had a recording of some of that. But when he missed the third gig, I had had enough. We broke up in July of 1965, after having played together for two years and two months.

This happened in Boston. Antonia and I were staying with Lowell "Banana" Levinger, who would go on to play with the Youngbloods, among many others, and Rick Turner, who would go on to found Alembic Guitars, providing instruments to the Grateful Dead. They were both 21. Antonia said she had not wanted to make musical suggestions while the Rounders were together, because it wasn't proper female behavior, despite the fact that we were her idea. But now that we had broken up, she felt it was ok. She was already high on speed, and although I hadn't had any in over a year, I took a big hit. We talked about music, specifically, among other things, the song "What's The Use Of Wondering", from *Oklahoma!*, to which she had made up some great new chords, which she showed me. I was very impressed, I had no idea she had such good music construction ideas. Then I showed her "You Done Me Wrong", the B-side of the Ray Price mega-hit "Crazy Arms", which I first heard in a bar in 1956. She immediately wrote new words to it, and it was transformed into "If You Want To Be A Bird." I was even more impressed. I had lost an epic musical partner, but found an epic new one.

Weber's Stinky Feet

Once upon a time, in 1964, Weber left his cowboy boots on all summer long while serially staying up for about five days in a row and crashing for three, which was his normal pattern for several years. Yes, he slept in them too. But one day, after three or four months, he took them off. Weber, Antonia and I shared a four-room railroad flat on Houston Street in the Lower East Side, half a block from the Parkside Lounge, which is still there. We were on one end, with the kitchen and the other room between us. But when he took them off, Antonia and I started gagging. We went to his room to see what the fuck. We saw. We had already smelled. We told him to put his boots on the fire escape and close the window. It was still unbearable. Then we told him to wash his feet in the tub. On he stunk. Finally, we brought him a can of Comet cleanser and told him to use it, which he did, scrubbing away for several minutes. Even that only worked a little bit. The bad smell lingered until the day after the next. Weber was a most singular human being. But he didn't treat his feet very well.

Weber The Human Hoop Snake

Back when Weber was living with me and Antonia, Weber would

often brag that he could blow himself. He said he learned a little yoga in high school to facilitate this. We kept saying, "Show us!" But he would just stomp off, growling. I drew a cartoon of a tent with a sign outside, "See Weber eat himself, 10 cents" (everything was cheaper back then), but he didn't think it was funny. But the years rolled, as they did, by, and in the early '70s there was a Rounder gig in Vermont. We weren't getting paid too much, and reedman Teddy Dean was trying to convince the owner to kick in some extra money after the gig.

"I mean, we're a real professional outfit! We deserve to be treated profess..." Teddy's voice trailed off as he saw the club manager's eyes shift to something behind him, his (the manager's) expression had become very odd. Teddy turned around. There was Weber lying down on the stage, trying to do the hoop snake. Only he was too drunk to get a hard-on. He was asking the women in the audience to join him on stage and assist him in this endeavor. No takers. Real professional outfit was our middle name.

A Story About 16-Year-Old Weber He Told Me When He Was 20

Weber, Antonia and I were listening to the radio. It played the 1960 Billy Vaughn instrumental hit, "Wheels". Weber said when that record came out, he had set off to hitchhike to California, from Bucks County, Pennsylvania. As luck would have it--as I said, he was always lucky--another teenager picked him up immediately. A very pissed-off teenager. He had just spent all his savings on a used car, and his parents went through the roof, insisting he return the car and get his money back. "Why listen to them?," Weber asked. "I'm going to California. Let's go to California, that'll show them!" Weber was killer handsome, and hugely charismatic. He had a genius for convincing people to do anything he asked. It didn't take much convincing. Off they went. The car radio played "Wheels". "See?," said Weber. "It's a sign!" Off they went in a fit of enthusiasm. As they wheeled away, the song kept them constant company. "It's our song!," said Weber. But by the time they hit the Western states, the driver was beginning to have misgivings. "Hey," said Weber, "you'll love California! A whole new life!" By the time they had crossed the Rockies, the car was start-ing to behave erratically. This increased as they wheeled on. I forget what part of California they ended up in, but by the time they got there, the car was dead and the kid was broke. "Thanks for the ride," said Weber, and off he went. We didn't ask him what he did out there. I wonder what he did out there.

Public Muse Abuser Number One

I never asked Weber if he believed he had a personal muse, but if he did, he wasn't very nice to her. I always believed I had one, who I saw as female. It's very weird, but very inevitable but very inevitable that Weber seemed to have no Muse. Mine was specific: I saw her as female. (Joni Mitchell saw hers as male; Tori Amos says she has eleven Muses.) My feelings toward the Muse are mainly awe, respect, gratitude, and fear. I have noticed that some musicians and mathe-maticians most inspired work happened when they were young. Their early work was their best work. There are few exceptions, like Jerome Kern. His first masterpiece, "They Didn't Believe Me", dates to 1914, and the brilliant "All Through The Day" was composed shortly before his death in 1946. His Muse never failed him, or he never failed his Muse. I have no idea what his attitude towards inspiration was. Irving Berlin did not believe in inspiration. He wrote about 1,500 songs. I had read that he wrote a song each evening after dinner. But if he wrote 1,500 songs over the 43 years he was active, that's about 35 a year. Most were duds. "I Wish Again I Was Back In Michigan" is no "How Deep Is The Ocean". But I digress.

Getting back to Weber's Muse abuse, let me count the ways. One is claiming you wrote a song that someone else had written. When we first met, Weber claimed to have written "Euphoria", and was telling people this during our performances. But one evening, Michael Hur-ley's sister was in the audience, and she went back to Buck's County, Pennsylvania, home of Weber, Michael Hurley, and Robin Remaily, and told Robin that Weber was claiming to have written "Euphoria". Robin, who I hadn't met yet, headed for New York with blood in his eyes. As it happened, Weber and I had just ingested a large number of peyote buttons, folks we hung out with favoring larger doses of hallucinogens back then. The drugs had firmly taken hold when I heard a knock on the door. It was Robin. He was wearing a dark green wool shirt with lighter green pockets and cuffs that had obviously been worn for years. "Wow," I said, "What a beautiful shirt!" With a smooth motion, he stripped it off and handed it to me, saying, "Take it, it's yours!" I had just met him, and he had given me the shirt off his back. What a guy! Then he confronted Weber in his room, and as the saying goes, tore him a new asshole.

However, Weber was soon composing. He made up two amazing guitar instrumentals, to which I eventually added words, marking our first and only collaborations, "Song Of Courtship To Dame Fortune" and "My Mind Capsized". Which brings us to the next variation on Muse abuse. Weber had been working on some songs by himself, but after gigs when we would be hanging with the crowd, Weber would pretend to be struck by inspiration. "I've got a new song, somebody write it down!" Someone, usually a girl, would find pen and paper, and take his dictation while Weber paced back and forth, hand to forehead, and repeat the words he had written days previously. His plan was to bask in the awe of the crowd watching him in the throes of inspiration. No one ever handed him pen and paper and said, "Write it down yourself." Everybody always wanted to do things for Weber. He would never have spare strings, and when his broke (usually the G) he would beseech the crowd to get him a new string. Everyone would run around saying, "Weber needs strings!," while Weber went through a number of poses I thought of as "boy damsel in distress". After this happened a few times I started bringing spare guitar strings to every gig.

After our break-up in 1965, he started writing songs. "One Will Do For Now" was a singular beauty with a structure like I've ever seen to this day. There are seven chords, and no chord repeats until all seven had been used. He also wrote the only Rounder hit ever (one that charted in Los Angeles and Washington DC): "Boobs A Lot". The song was almost lost, Weber made it up on the spot when he was still with the Fugs, and would have forgotten it if Tuli Kupferberg hadn't written it down. During this time he also wrote "Generalonely" and

"Half A Mind". I thought the songs, "One Will Do For Now" and "Half A Mind" were (among other things) about how the two of us, which was sort of an entity, weren't one anymore. The songs seemed to mourn our breakup. I told that to Weber once, and he said he hadn't thought of that. Weber wasn't very good about thinking of anyone but himself.

His original songs became more few and further between. In the '70s and '80s, he didn't write any that I was aware of. In the '90s he wrote just two of them, the best one, "Who's Your Momma", he wrote while on crack. He would periodically throw out a beginning, never to finish it. Or act weird if something was finished. When we were working on our *Too Much Fun* album in Bucks County, he started making up this song about living on Monkey Island. I immediately joined him, and a whole amazing song got made up. Jane Gilday was there, recording us, and the song was saved! I was delighted--we had a new Weber song for the album! But he didn't want to record it, or even try to sing it again, and wouldn't give me a reason why. A couple years later he was partying with a girlfriend on Halloween, and, as he told me later, made up these five great songs. I asked to hear them. He said they weren't finished yet. He just played me part of one. It was called, "Who's Knife?". The POV character has just been stabbed in a knife fight, and the knife was on the floor. "Who's knife is that?" the POV character keeps asking, while bleeding to death. That's all I remember, he only sang it that once. It was a real good start. A year later, he again started making up a song. I offered to write it down, but he was singing it and I couldn't write the words as fast as he sang them. I asked him to sing it again so I could get more of the lyrics transcribed. He was disgruntled, but did it again, a noticeably inferior version. I got a few more of the words, though. I asked him to do it again, and he wouldn't. That's when I gave up on giving a damn about his songs.

But then there was the art show he had at Ed Sanders' Peace Eye Book Store (And Scrounge Lounge). The only piece I remember was a radio he had rigged to play all the stations at once. He called it, "Babylon". Oh, Weber! The things he could have done. The songs he could have written. The arms he could have spared the needle. The brain he could have left un-fried. He was as fun to watch as a herd of gazelles back in the day. Never was there anyone like him. Never will there be again. That he even happened once is beyond unbelievable. If I had to choose having a life with Weber in it to having had one without, I'd have one with, please. Hands down. And Antonia's plan to keep Weber off the streets? It worked. That being said, Weber definitely peaked just before the Beatles hit, and the following decades of his life were a bumpy downhill slide of hard drugs, alcoholism, abuse of friends and fellow musicians combined with moments of true connection and inspiration that kept his friends and fellow musicians from leaving him. For the last several decades of his life, Weber needed a "handler" in order to function musically, or at all. On the flip side, there was always someone willing to be that person. He was so outside the norm that he was kind of like a one-man circus-- endlessly entertaining for audiences, as long as they didn't have to shovel the elephant shit.

PETER STAMPFEL in THE BOSTON BROADSIDE, 1964 to 1967

In 1964, the Rounders were playing in Boston and Dave Wilson asked if I would like to write a column for the local, folkcentric periodical *Broadside*. I asked, "Does it pay?" I don't know if he said, "No, but you'll get a lot of exposure," but he definitely said, "No." However, the prospect of thrusting my views on hundreds, maybe even thousands, was immediately enticing. So 49 times over the next three years, I smoked some weed and wrote first drafts in ballpoint pen. I used to think those first drafts were more genuine or something— like the often-true recording studio cliche: first take, best take. Back then I even considered overdubbing a kind of cheating. Whatta dummy. It took me a while to understand that writing is basically re-writing, often re-re-re-writing.

Anyway, somebody had the job of deciphering my sloppy writing of my final draft. I'm told they really hated doing it. Many typos ensued. With the help of Benito Vila, who also copyedited my 40,000-some words for the 100-song project, I cleaned up the columns that needed it most, deleted some dumb shit I said (here and there) and added some comments from the present, which are set off by <angle brackets>. On wise advice, I PC'd a few things. For example, Negro has been changed to Black. Back then, Negro was the acceptable word and Black would have been considered derogatory. Times change and so do words. You'll find "chicks", which is what the girls were called. Guys were cats. All the cats and chicks got their kicks at the hop. And by taking drugs. After July of 1965, many of my columns were written on speed. By the time the column ended, I was subsequently beginning to lose my teeth. Ah, stupid youth.

Bear in mind I wrote these between the ages of 24 and 27, and was frequently a cranky twerp. Still, here are my contributions to Broadside, my encouragement of good living and real listening. I ended up deleting very little. Most of it held up better than I thought it might. These are all period pieces from a more innocent time, captured fairly well, if I can say so. Help yourself to a steaming pile of yesterdays. Enjoy! Wipe your shoes off afterwards.

1964 as HOLYMODAL BLITHER

Volume III, No. 9 • June 24, 1964

The following will be random prejudices dealing with what is called folk music. Sometimes I will lie by mistake and other times I will lie on purpose or for the hell of it. Perhaps on occasion I will contradict myself or do an annotated article on ice cube sucking. But mostly, this will be a kick-your-shoes-off homespun schizophrenic dialogue, Great God, concerning those ever-popular concepts:

Folk
And
Music.

Ah yes, folk music. I will define my terms because that's a good starting place.

Folk is people, music is organized noise; thus, organized people noises. And yet more specific; first off, can just anyone be a folk? or do you have to have calluses? A lot of people seem to feel that "folk" means lower class and/or lower middle class. These people used to be called "working class" and are the people who a few hundred years ago were illiterate. So all their tradition was, you know, oral...Anyway, this group comprises 80% of the population of our country. And what of the other 20%? Hah?

The song "Waly Waly" was supposedly written by a member of royalty, which establishes a precedent. If royalty can write folk songs, then royalty are folk, too.

"Take that, royalty. Now you're a folk like everybody else."
"How dare you, you young jackanapes!"
"Gee, Maw, it's a classless society."
"Eat your grits, Jed."
"And we're all just folks."
"That's plain talk, Jed. Eat your grits".

Now we know we can all be folks, even if our mommies and daddies are rich. So much for folk.

As for music, songs and tunes and whistles and hums and chants and football cheers are all music. Some people talk pure music all the time. A large amount of the noises made by the animal kingdom are music. I should think it would be easier to make music when you make noise than not. In fact I believe everyone could make music all the time and still get things done if they wanted to. Yes, I believe everyone could get things done better. We could all have Natural Rhythm and bop around balancing pots of water on our heads.

Then there's noises made by non-human sources. When is it music and when is it not? By me the wind is music, and thunder, and the noise my refrigerator is making right now, and dripping faucet noises...

So as far as the medium goes there's plenty of room. Folk music in the particular sense is simply anything anyone calls folk music. The idea is based on the idea that everyone has a different view of reality and everyone's view of reality is equally valid. Thus:

1. Folk is anyone.
2. Music is any sound.
3. Folk music is any sound anyone calls folk music.

Next issue I will get more specific.

Volume III, No. 10 - NATURAL RHYTHM EXPOSED • July 8, 1964

Natural rhythm is a real thing like gravity. City people who are civilized don't usually have any. That is what being civilized means to a certain extent.

Natural rhythm comes from nature, of course, which country people are closer to. So they have more natural rhythm from watching the plants grow, the beasts in the field, etc. So country people tend to keep the beat better.

Often city people who play folk music, however, can't keep the beat because they have no natural rhythm to help them and they go faster and faster. This is called rushing, and is bad. If you rush a lot, the gypsies will steal you and make you drink goat's milk.

To get natural rhythm is hard but not impossible. Ask any jazz musician. *<That was the go-to response on where to find drugs. I was making a joke.>* Try watching pile drivers. Observe the great starry wheels in the sky and how they spin. Pay attention to the phases of the moon and the passing seasons. Listen to your heart beat. Soon you will have natural rhythm. But not for sure. The modern world is very uncertain.

Other ways to get natural rhythm. Eat a lot of prunes. Blow your nose regularly. Boil plenty of water. Take drugs.

Volume III, No. 11 • July 22, 1964

Blind Cripple Lush. People say, "Ever hear of Blind Cripple Lush?," and I say, "Sure." He was my pal, ol' pal. There was such a man. Carried his guitar in a gunny sack. He was real, although he wasn't truly blind, or actually a cripple. Sure was a lush, though. With a natural talent for self-branding. Me and Blind Cripple used to hitchhike and drink wine in low places, whistle at girls, eat soda crackers and roll on the ground. It was heaven on Earth.

<Eat soda crackers and roll on the ground is a line from an old hillbilly song called, "Big Balls in Nashville". I would introduce it as a song about a courageous Tennessean's struggle with elephantiasis—the enlargement and hardening of limbs or body parts, a disease often resulting in testicles larger than watermelons.>

"Lush," I asked him, "What do you think of all those commercial people who go around wearing madras Bermuda shorts and driving motorscooters, and then they play folk music? Huh, Lush?"

He stared at a girl at the end of the bar and picked his nose.

"They suck," he replied evenly.

<When I wrote this back in 1964, I hadn't seen the phrase he, she, it or they suck in print anywhere. My search for the earliest printed example was fruitless. So maybe I got there first. Kinda doubt it though.>

Then he went to the bathroom to throw up. He knew how to be humble.

He wasn't too proud to beg. He used to go up to, you know, those guys in their, you know, suits and ties, and say, "Buddy, can you spare a dime?" And they'd look at him, and a couple of times even I saw him get a quarter. Then he'd buy some more wine. He was infested with vermin a lot, but, hell, aren't we all in some way or other, you know what I mean.

Blind Cripple was a folksinger's folksinger. A man's man. A lush's lush.

Volume III, No. 13 • August 19, 1964

These will be splinters--paragraphs is perhaps a clearer word--not intending to relate to each other, but they probably will of their own accord. Things often do.

"Who will solve our problems now that there's no N.R.A.?" (1930s 78-rpm record)

A couple of months ago, I lauded the famous Folkways Anthology Of American Folk Music, which was six LP records comprising 84 selections, each being lambent and crunchy. There are also 84 basic yoga positions. I could see--before 1970--a doctoral thesis on the relation of the successive yoga positions to the corresponding tracks on the Anthology.

1984 is 20 years away.

Some people's names should be in print more. John Fahey! John Fahey! John Fahey! Shape note hymns tear me up. I'd like to be a shape note hymn.

The more I hear the Rolling Stones the more I like them.

Most of the Dylan copiers would have been Bob Gibson copiers in 1961 and Pete Seeger copiers in 1958. Bob Gibson was a Pete Seeger copier in 1958.

I have recently been lent all seven of the Original Jazz Library records. Two are of Charley Patton, one is of Henry Thomas, one is of women *<I actually said "chicks">*, two are assorted country blues, and one is jug bands. Got the assorted country blues, great god!

I don't want to hear 12-bar blues anymore. I got the 12-bar blues, 'cause the changes never change. Prefer exotic and irregular country blues. Much prefer. Grunt.

"Trains are a gas. Umbrellas are a drag."—Dino Valente

"You take the table, and I'll take the chairs."—Country song about divorce, 1960 or so.

When things are written about in country songs, you know those things have reached the lowest common denominator. And look! There he is! The Lowest Common Denominator his own self!

LCD: "Call me Low".

"Gee, Low, it sure is good to know that you're around to have things get down to. It makes me feel kind of secure, you know?"

"That's mighty pleasin' to my ears," said Low.

"Cause when things get down to you," I explained. "Everybody knows about it and you can talk to anybody about it."

"Mighty pleasin'," said Low.

"Lots of things have made it down to you already, like Debbie Reynolds and Stalin, and hub caps, and Coca Cola."

"Yup, yup, I recollect each one."

"And I think it's just swell of you to wait here so patiently with your Cosmic Catcher's Mitt..."

"Look out!," yelled Low. I ducked into a convenient ditch. There was a loud splat that sounded like a concept landing in a Cosmic Catcher's Mitt. The sound was similar to that of the men working on the chain. But in a nice way.

After the Second World War and Korea, thousands of one-hundred-percent American boys came home married to foreign women. It took awhile for the general public to get used to this, but songs like "Fraulein" and "Geisha Girl" signified acceptance. And being country music, there were a host of copy songs, like, "My Filipino Baby" and "She's My Eskimo Pie".

"In a moment of glory a face shines before me, the face of my pretty fraulein."

"It's written in the tea leaves, and it's written in the sand. I found love by the heart-full in a far and distant land. Tell the old folks that I'm happy with someone who's true I know. I love my pretty geisha girl where the ocean breezes blow."

Splat!, and an enemy is forgiven.

See how easy?

The river of rebellion is overflowing and the onion patch is in big trouble. Treat consumers with respect during the remainder of the evening. THEN WE STRIKE!

An army of long time men will patrol the onion patch, feeling bad. Sleep will be impossible. Terms of any kind will not be discussed until group A meets group B in the service center. Next, we get vocal. The NEW CHRISTY MINSTRELS will be lurking behind a hedge disguised as quaint Mexican laborers, who had just had their names taken away so they can ride the big airplane. At a preplanned signal, they whip out polystyrene ukuleles and chant:

Pestilence and poverty!
Earwax and lobotomy!
Make a social-conscience man feel bad
Poor boy

At once the Hootenanny Army of Patent Rebellion is on the attack. We march through the orchards of California, commenting loudly at the amount of rotten fruit lying on the ground. Next, we fly a jet to Kentucky to see the oppressed miners go underground. We present them with stockings the hootenanny girls knitted on flight. Time for shopping and sightseeing will be provided.

The hootenanny army is advised to talk to the folk whenever possible. Conversation can be opened with a simple gambit like, "I haven't eaten meat in three days" or "Can I sleep in your barn tonight, mister?" It doesn't matter if the folks you're talking to don't have a barn. Contact is what counts. If too much difficulty is met in the field of provisions, feel free to rob nearby orchards. The fruit probably will rot on the ground anyway.

Volume III, No. 15 • September 30, 1964

It is interesting to see how contemporary nonfolkmusic and folkmusic look at each other. For instance, a few months ago, I heard a "Folk Music" record by a rock & roll group called the Four Seasons. The Four Seasons are one of the best groups going; every record they have released since 1962 has made the top ten. One of the many things this group has going for them is an almost mindless hysterical joy...

Sha-aa-aa ay ay ay ayaree bay-ay bee
(Sherry baby)
Sha-aa-ree, won't you come out tonight

(Come, come, come out tonight)

I mean mindless in the way an animal moves, un-hung up.

That song I just paraphrased was called "Sherry" and came out in 1962. It just so happened that at the time the village was full of girls named Sherry, most of whom, for some reason, were dykes. So everywhere in the village where there was a jukebox, someone would be playing "Sherry". The following conversation was common:

"Hey, have you seen Sherry around?"
"Which Sherry?"
"You know, dyke Sherry."
"Which dyke Sherry?"

Anyway, a few months ago I heard a couple cuts from a folk music record by the Four Seasons. The songs I heard were new ones, and just what you would expect. Lonesome roads, midnight trains, and plenty of suffering. Shame on the Four Seasons.

But really, their angle of attack was the usual one for people to take concerning folk music.

Most people consider folk music more serious than ordinary music, and when seriousness is required, most people start to take themselves seriously. This is always a terrible mistake.

This taking yourself seriously business is responsible for the vast amount of contemporary folk songs dealing with lonesome travelling, dirty old bombs, nasty old fallout, and the cruel civil war.

Cannonball don't pay no mind
If you're gentle, if you're kind
Honey, let me be your salty dog.

There's a bunch of paradoxes around here. For example, almost all of the people who sing about rambling around and not giving damns for greenback dollars are making plenty of money and flying in jets. Why doesn't someone make up a folksong about making plenty of money and flying in jets?

But the thing that bothers me most about these songs is the awful drone of self-pity that runs through them. The idea of all these young people (most people who buy folk music records are young people) indulging in bizarre fantasies in which they are long-gone, lean, hungry, hard-traveling men of constant sorrow--damn it, self-pity is so negative, and besides, it's chickenshit.

While I'm complaining, there's another thing that's been on my mind. That is, how much I don't like the versions of "Blowin' in the Wind" done by Stan Getz and Lena Horne. Getz is a brilliant musician, and there's little more I can say. What can you say about a first rate artist besides that he's a first rate artist without becoming redundant? But his "Blowin' in the Wind" sounds like Billy Vaughn. And Lena Horne's version...Oh, well, I just don't care for big bands and 1940s-style arrangements. *<But as the years went by, I came to love them. Some of them, at least.>*

A few days ago, Weber and I worked opposite one of those new christy style groups. I had never seen one of these groups in action before and had been wondering for some time why they were so popular. Revelation! One of the things people like best about folk music is that most folksingers are young and rather pretty. And they're so active...the way they stamp their feet, clap their hands and swing their guitar necks over the microphone.

This cracked on me in 1962, when I was living in Chicago. I was putting down a folksinging group because I didn't think they were very good, and an older friend of mine said that they weren't very good, but they looked so nice, young, active, intelligent...And anyway, most people don't listen very closely, they just watch. Well, if people like to look at a couple of young, pretty, active people, they'll like looking at a young, pretty, active crowd even better. As they do.

People who perform traditional folk music tend to not be concerned with the showmanship angle of being on stage and focus on the music. But there's nothing wrong with "showmanship" and all that. Like anything else, it depends on how it's used. So I thought up a planned, organized setting for traditional folk music that would please a larger segment. Ain't nothing like pleasing larger segments

The curtain rises.

Nine young ladies dressed as attendant dancers to the goddess Cybele file across the stage waving censers which are full of burning incense and other things. The fumes fill the audience. A flashing neon sign is lowered from the ceiling which reads:

Orville Swamp Bucket

and

Prescott Dregs

A small boy dressed in a 1940s Hollywood version of a pioneer kid costume runs across the stage, rolling a hoop, shouting, "Gee whillikers, Maw. It's a string band."

The string band plays first selection, after which a woman dressed in Hollywood style pioneer chick costume runs widdershins around the string band, shouting, "Chase them away, Henry! They've come to molest the livestock."

Background noises from offstage: MOO! WHINNY NEIGH! BOW WOW! QUACK QUACK! COCK A DOODLE DOO! BAAA! MEOW! CLUCK CLUCK!

Next, the string band plays "Come little Suzy, let's go up to the loft, the hay up there is always warm and soft", etc., after which black-eyed Suzy, played by Debbie Reynolds, wearing a fetishy milkmaid costume and 6-inch spike cowboy boots, says, "Sure."

Pioneer mother shouts, "Do something, Henry. My dander is getting riled."

Henry appears from the wings, dressed American gothic, and says, "Stop talking so dumb, Maw. I can't do a thing unless I get high first."

"Shucks, Henry, you can always score from a string band."

"The very thing!" Henry runs toward the string band, screaming, "What's happening, Jack! What's happening, Jack!"

String band slips Henry a plain manila envelope and plays final selection.

The curtain descends.

Dwight D. Eisenhower presents the string band with a golden record. The string band presents Eisenhower with a silver dagger. Betty Furness presents the audience with a paper of pins, comfits, doctored Coca Cola, hallucinogenic barnacles, and glow-in-the-dark statues of Charlie Poole seducing an allegorical figure representing avarice, Peoria, Illinois, and Tuesday afternoons in February.

Audience goes: MOO! WHINNY! NEIGH! BOW WOW! QUACK QUACK! COCK A DOODLE DOO! BAAA! MEOW! CLUCK CLUCK!

The string band plays encore. Publisher of the National Inquirer, who happened to be in the audience, announces that starting next issue, he will print nothing but hardcore pornography.

Audience: YAY! HOORAY!

Audience files out. Everyone has beatific visions all the way home.

<Some time after this column appeared, a guy I knew vaguely came up to me and said he wanted to buy "a trey of smack", which he thought was a cool

way of saying three dollars worth of heroin.

"What the fuck are you talking about?," I said.
"You can always score from a string band," he explained, referring to this column.

"That was a joke!," I said. I'm not a dealer, for crissake!

"Come on, man," he said, "I want to buy a trey of smack."

Ay yi yi.>

Volume III, No. 18 • November 11, 1964

Among, ha-ha, traditional folk music circles, everyone takes it for granted that one works out one's own musical arrangement or copies some traditional one. Copying traditional arrangements is, of course, how you learn how to play traditional folk music.

But, the majority of professional folk singers are incapable of working out their own arrangements. So they have other people do their arrangements for them. These people are usually professional arrangers who don't know much about traditional folk music. The same arrangers frequently arrange rock'n roll for professional rock'n roll singers who are incapable of working out their own arrangements. Because many arrangers have been working on rock'n roll for almost ten years, a lot of them have gotten very good indeed.

The rock'n roll/rhythm and blues artists who have the greatest popularity, however, are the ones who do their own arrangements and write a lot of their own songs. For example, Fats Domino, Ray Charles, Little Richard, Chuck Berry, The Four Seasons and the Beatles.

The longer folk music is around, the more selective people will become concerning it. History is on our side. And the taste of the early teen group that buys so many records keeps improving. Not to mention the taste of children. In the Lower East Side, where I live, there are a lot of young people singing in the streets by ones, twos, or in groups...singing with strange harmonies!...some of them seven or eight years old!...really singing together!...interestingly!...little girls singing Beatle songs and getting all the notes right! Things are getting very strange very quickly.

By now, most of you have probably noticed the development of the old-timey costume. As far as I can make out, it started in the late '50s, when leather, vests, and boots started becoming popular, the old Boho work shirt being concurrent with the peasant look for girls.

Take those little wire shades, for example. Several women's magazines were touting them last summer. The first guy who I heard of wearing them was Steve Weber in 1962. The old-timey costume is having more of an influence on popular fashions. There is nothing remarkable about this development: American styles have always been inspired mainly by foreigners, Bohemians, Blacks and homosexuals--also musicians and prostitutes--simply because these groups are more inventive in their way of dressing than most Americans.

The Beatles and the Rolling Stones are in a related clothing scene. As an example, look at the outward similarity in the appearance of the Rolling Stones and Kweskin's Jug Band. Naturally, you or I could tell them apart six blocks away, but as far as most people are concerned, "They all look alike." Like Blacks and Beatniks. The coming thing is a combination of the Beatles' look and the old-timey look.

<Note the Sergeant Pepper look three years later.>

The world sure is getting strange.

<But I had no idea how strange it would become.>

Whenever I've been in Boston, many people have asked where I learned those songs and "where do you hear music like that?" The main place I found out about traditional American folk music was listening to the Folkways Anthology of American Folk Music, which is six LP records containing 84 selections, all taken from old (1925–1933) 78-rpm records. The records are put out by Folkways. The serial numbers are FA2951 (a-b), FA295 1 (c-d), FP252, FP253, FA2952, FA2953.

Anyway, buy all these records. Play them all the time, for years. They will probably sound strange at first. (The first time I heard one of the records, I went on a hysterical laughing and rolling-on-the-floor jag, which lasted at least ten minutes.) After a few hearings, you'll get used to them. Read the accompanying booklet, which has the Grand Monochord of the Universe on its cover, which is funny as hell.

<The booklet is funny, not the Grand Monochord. Eventually, I was one of the people who wrote the liner notes for the CD re-issue. Even got a Grammy for that.>

In closing, these records have changed my life. And a lot of other people's, too. This was, in fact, Harry Smith's original intention.

<Bob Dylan has said, "If not for the Smith Anthology, there wouldn't be a Bob Dylan.">

That's how good they are. I wish these records would be played constantly in every American home.

1965

Volume III, No. 22 • January 6, 1965

Records are one of the best things. Today I was lying down and listening to records a lot. I thought about how recently this had been possible, no recordings until the 1890s, no extended play records until the 1940s, no 45-RPMs until the '50s. Things are great now, though. Plenty good records around.

I'm going to go on about records. Black shiny flat disks. I decided I don't want to write about bad records anymore. There is so much trash about, especially in the folk field. (The Bobbsey Twins and Their Hydraulic Folk Field. "Turn on the power, Bert," said Nan. His clean-cut features were aglow with interest.)

<The Boobsey Twins, featuring Bert and Nan, was a popular early 20th-century children's book series.>

Anyway, it's too easy to pick up a record, Accordion Band Favorites or something, and say, what garbage, or something. So I decided to just talk about records I like. Besides, with the ever increasing number of records coming out, I could spend all my time just talking about records I like. And neglecting a friend to berate a foe is a terrible waste of time.

Records. We've all had experiences of listening to old 78-RPM records on a windup Victrola. What a great word Victrola is! My mother told me that when she was a little girl, she and her friend would play "The Letter Edged In Black" over and over while sitting under a blanket covered card table and cry and cry. That was in northern Wisconsin in the 1920s.

In the 1940s in southern Wisconsin, my cousin and I used to listen to a Victrola that had been painted with an incredible shade of cream that almost all the wood surfaces in almost all the kitchens in Milwaukee were painted in the 1930s and '40s. A rich in butterfat but slightly dirty cream. The color always made me a little sick.

The Victrola was in my cousin's basement, along with boxes of comic books, hockey sticks, and boxing gloves. There were only a few records, an instrumental of "Wang Wang Blues", a patriotic hillbilly record from World War Two, and a few others I've forgotten. But the best one of all was an old German children's record that was on the wrong speed no matter how you adjusted it. It was at least twice as fast as it should have been. Maybe some records used a different speed in Germany. Whenever it would play, I would have a hysterical laughing fit and roll on the floor, which unnerved my cousin.

The voice on the record was that of an old German grand-mother, or someone who sounded like one, telling a fairy tale. All the spaces between the words and the words themselves seemed to be equal, giving them a staccato feel. The background music, played over and over, was "Morning", from Peer Gynt Suite, and it was going at triple speed, sounding like a merry-go-round out of control. They played it at Luther Burbank School in 1948 during a school show. All the Kindergarteners were dressed up like flowers, as if they were all waking up in the morning. Spike Jones, one of my childhood idols as well as one of my adult idols, did a version of it as well. I loved that he often fired a pistol in the middle of a piece of music.

I mentioned a patriotic hillbilly song from the Second World War. There was one called "There's A Star Spangled Banner Waving Some-where", which moved me deeply when I was four or five years old. I remember standing on the porch of my other cousin's house while we were saying good-bye, and looking at the stars, which seemed to be unusually bright. You could always see lots of stars back then. About twice when I was looking at the stars, that song came on the radio. The feeling I got seemed to come from the song, but it was really about the way the stars looked. I remember very little of the words: "God gave me the right to be a true American, and American is what I'll always be". The important thing about all this is how I felt while listening to the song and looking at the stars.

<About ten years after I wrote this I finally got hold of the words, intending to sing it. But they were awful. Beyond awful, even. The person singing wants to be a soldier, and "take Hitler down a peg", but can't get drafted because he is "a cripple". I think the word here is mawkish.>

Volume IV, No. 4 • April 15, 1965

Commercial! Commercial!

Now, here is how you can buy the incredible, interesting, inspir-ing record "Death Chants, Breakdowns, and Military Waltzes," by John Fahey!

"What's on the record?," you ask. A perfectly fair question.

Music! Real music!

All the selections on the record are instrumental. All are solo guitar except one band which is guitar and flute. Some of the tunes are traditional but the majority were made up by Fahey.

One thing there has been much dearth of: that's good new tunes in folk music. About the only people I know making up tunes without the same old chords and progressions are Steve Weber and John Fahey. It is such a pleasure to hear good new tunes fingerpicked on guitar. Fingerpicked guitar is one of my favorite sounds in the world, and Fahey fingerpicks brilliantly. His technique is solid and perfect. He has taste! And taste and folk music are not usually very close.

Fahey's record is a record to live with, play a lot, listen to first thing in the morning, and play several times in a row.

People who already have the record tend to consider it one of their favorite possessions. People who have played the record many, many times say they keep hearing things which they never noticed before. This is because Fahey (unlike most people in folk music) is a complicated person and it shows in his work. Any tune on the record can be listened to on dozens of levels.

To get more information on this record, write to Takoma Records, Box 2233, South Berkeley Station, Berkeley 3, California. Send today and make yourself happy!

Volume IV, No. 5 • April 28, 1965

I've been interested in the current use of the word "soul", so I'm going to go on about that. I'll do that in essay fashion; it's easier that way.

Blacks are responsible for most of the musical developments that have happened in America. One reason is because during most of America's history, Black musicians have been less concerned with musical limitations than their White counterparts.

The reason American fiddling is so different from the Anglo-European fiddling upon which it is based is that Blacks invented the style in the 1700s. Maybe the 1600s. Blacks also invented the five-string banjo, which was based on an African instrument, and are responsible for the development of most pre-Scruggs-style five-string banjo techniques. In fact, most pre-World War Two hillbilly instrumental techniques were pioneered by Black musicians as long ago as the early nineteeth century.

Around 1900 many Black musicians started picking up on guitar in preference to banjo or fiddle. Guitars in large numbers had been brought back by the mostly lower class soldiers returning from the Spanish-American War. A natural choice—the guitar had more possibilities.

Now white musicians have been copying Black musicians since the early 1800s. As a rule, the White musicians were a long way behind the musicians they were copying, often decades behind. This lag is on-going and I believe it is permanent.

<What follows is a theory I had, or that I got from others, I don't remember which. It has a simplistic, semi-crackpot air, but I decided to leave it in for better or for worse. But I did toss a bunch of clueless misinformation from this column.>

During the '40s, many Black musicians, especially younger ones, embraced the concept of "cool". The whole idea of COOL is very complex, but simply put: 1. being cool was partly a reaction against Whites popular image of the Black; 2. being cool was the popular Black image of what being White was. But by the 1940s, many whites were trying to copy the cool attitude. And the spectacle of Whites-copying-Blacks-copying-Whites made a lot of folks start to think, "Hey, wait..."

Getting back to my starting point which was SOUL. The first time I heard that word used in the current way was around 1958, in reference to the music of Ray Charles. Soul was used in preference to Rhythm and Blues, because in 1958 Rhythm and Blues and Rock'n Roll were largely, by most people, considered TRASH. But by 1958, it was becoming clear to most people that Ray Charles was in no way trash. In other words, Soul was a positive synonym for Rhythm and Blues. Quickly it became used to cover, in a positive way, all the facets of Black popular culture.

But the thing that made me start this whole business is the way in which the word "soul" has been frequently used for a little while now. It's taken on a whiner's approach, perfectly typified by the following line from a Ben E. King song called "7 Letters":

This is my 7th letter baby
I just can't write you any more
My poor little fingers swole---

"My poor little fingers swole"! Can you imagine a grown man saying that! And every time someone on the radio has said "soul" in relation to a record for the last year or so, the record has been a self-pitying wallow.

Soul is a much nicer word than that.

Volume IV, No. 7 • May 26, 1965

Popular music has gone through immense changes in the last few years--specifically since 1962.

The main thing that happened in 1962 was that that was the first year since 1958 that the majority of popular songs were good songs. I had stopped listening to pop music in January 1959, the death of Buddy Holly, the Big Bopper and Richie Valens was the last straw. Previous straws being Little Richard quitting rock n' roll and joining the Church, and Chuck Berry and Jerry Lee Lewis being kicked off the radio--Chuck Berry for bringing an under-age girl across state lines and Jerry Lee Lewis marrying his 13-year old cousin. Yeah, and there was also Elvis getting drafted, but by then I was no longer a big fan.

Then there was the fact that the Italian mob controlled a lot of the pop music industry. They were driven nuts by White girls going crazy for Black musicians. So by 1959, they were introducing a raft of nice Italian boys, like Fabian. Once in a while after that, I would play a rhythm and blues station or a country station, but mostly I listened to records.

Of course there were always good records coming out, like "Stay", by Maurice Williams and the Zodiacs, and "I Danced 'Til a Quarter to Three", by Gary U.S. Bonds, which I caught on the jukebox, but I ignored pop radio until late 1962. Suddenly, I found the majority of the records they were playing were good. Sure, they still had Connie Francis and Bobby Vinton (the queen and king of melodic barf), but there was also the Four Seasons, the Miracles, Mary Wells, the Chiffons, the Crystals and the Shirelles. That was the second big surprise: all of a sudden there were all these good girl groups. Pop singers had traditionally been male about 90 % of the time.

Since 1962, I have been saying most pop records are good, but I never made an actual count until a month or so ago. I counted all the songs in the top 100, categorizing them A (I 'd play it on the jukebox), B (I don't mind listening to it), or C (I can't stand it). About 33% of the records in the top 100 were in class A, almost half were in class B, and a scant 20% were in class C. However, in the top 30, there were only five records I couldn't stand: a Connie Francis, a Dean Martin, that "Red Roses for a Blue Lady" thing, and two others.

As a rule, the top third of the top 100 has a higher percentage of good ones and English ones than the bottom third. In a recent list, 15 out of the first 30 records were English.

We were just in Syracuse--a small, paranoid town--but it had some fine radio stations. One of them kept playing a public service announcement, telling you to investigate charities before you give to them because many of them are crooked. And the announcement has a great modern rock instrument behind it, so it was fun to hear. Also heard a new Coca-Cola ad by Jan and Dean that was good, and there's that great Coke ad by the Shirelles with a funny talking part. The Shirelles are blowing this riff about "Who took my Coke?" and "Coke is what's happening, baby." The previous Coke ad was by the Gateway Singers and it sounded like they were saying, "Life is much more fun when you're repressed." They were saying "refreshed" but it sure sounded like repressed to me.

1962 was a very sudden year. There was the Cuban missile crisis. The world was supposed to come to an end in February. Greenwich Village, for the first time, took on a 42nd Street character, and it became hip, too, for 18-year olds to panhandle. I had never heard anyone say "spare change" until then. This happened almost simultaneously in North Beach and Greenwich Village. This was also the year the first 12-and-13-year old runaways started to show up on the scene.

I can remember when all the chicks in all the ads in all the women's magazines turned me off. 1962 was the first year that more than half of them turned me on.

But in 1962, I considered 1962 a very bad year. Most people I knew had very bad things happen to them. And a lot of people recognized it was a strange year by late fall. By that time, people in California were calling it "the year of the ax."

Volume IV, No. 8 • June 9, 1965

Lately a lot of people have been telling me things about Bob Dylan. Not about his music, but about things he was supposed to have done, or neglected to do. Hey, did you hear that Dylan keeps a container of toe jam in his guitar case for luck?

Stories about contemporary folksingers amuse me. They seldom get nasty, I've noticed, until the folksinger in question is doing well financially. I started hearing Joan Baez stories in 1961. My favorite, which I heard from two different people, was that she had just married Duane Eddy. I heard my first Dylan story in 1962: He was going to play Holden Caulfield in a movie version of *Catcher In The Rye*.

My first experience with folk defamations was in 1958. A friend of mine, Rob Hunter, was making up dirty stories about a certain Nashville banjo player's questionable affection for livestock, especially mules. It was a natural thing to do, there we were in Milwaukee, 19 years old, and our mind's had been totally copped by hillbilly/country music for a little over a year. So Rob was making up these stories about this banjo player, none of these stories, so far as he knew, being true. People go to curious extremes to amuse themselves.

These stories occupied us for a few days, and supplied us with some new standing jokes. Then we moved on. Later that year I drove my '46 Ford coupe to San Francisco, and learned to play banjo in Compton, California.

Anyway, when I got to New York in 1959, one of the first things I heard was the story Rob had made up about the banjo player and his mule girl friends. Some Bronx kid told it to me and he swore it was true. I told him, "Don't be silly, my friend made that up," but he didn't believe me.

New York was buzzing with rumors. Charlie Poole was a lush. (True, as it turned out) Other rumors had him as a coke-head. Most of these rumors were pure speculation. Charlie Poole was a bondage enthusiast. The rumors were understandable, here are these people you don't know much about, and most of them have been dead for some time. Charlie Poole stole a biplane in Arkansas.

There were also rumors about seemingly successful contemporary folksingers, usually derogatory first person, as in, I saw so-and-so kick a dog, or second person, my friend saw so-and-so kick a dog.

But then everyone's done something put-down worthy at some time or other. All the dumb things I've ever done would make a heap of nasty stories, not to mention the things I did that looked bad from the outside, but really weren't too bad. Most people do several stupid things every day. Many people's lives are a series of nonstop stupid things. Most of us are pretty messed up. During the Middle Ages, churchmen estimated the odds of someone going to heaven as between one in a hundred thousand and one in a million. This during a time when most people in Europe saw no more than 200 different human beings in the course of their lives.

It would be easy and maybe even appropriate to bring up the Bible thing about casting stones, but I never read the Bible except for the first paragraph, The Song of Solomon, and the Book of Revelations. Nevertheless, there is a temptation to draw a moral and stop. But that would be so old-fashioned.

GROPE FOR PEACE!

Volume IV, No. 9 • June 23, 1965

There's this new product that Weber loves that comes in a spray can and it's silicone-based. You spray it on your guitar neck and your fingers slip and slide with slick ease. If you spray some on your guitar neck or ukulele neck or whatever, it feels viscous, yet dry. It costs $1.50 and music-selling stores should have it. You can spray it on your doorknobs, too. Use your imagination.

The Rolling Stones sure play good.

Things are being done so that John Fahey is coming to Boston this summer. There are many new Fahey tunes. I've been hearing about one called "The Dance of Death" that's supposed to be one of the best yet. He will be playing with his chick, who I've heard plays as good as he does. She sings lead and he sings harmony. I think they're going to work as Mr. and Mrs. John Fahey.

Besides Corn Flakes and Strawberries, there's a cereal with bananas called "Banana Whackies" or something, but I haven't tried it yet. I like honey on cereal better than sugar on cereal.

Just heard the original version of "Louie, Louie", by Richard Berry. It's better.

We've been staying at the Trolls' house in Boston. The Trolls hang upside down and their place is full of wires and musical instruments. It's great. You just fall over and there's something to play.

<There were three Trolls: Lowell Levinger, aka Banana, who went on to play with the Youngbloods; Rick Turner, who was working on his first-ever guitar neck and later went on to found Alembic Guitars, building instruments for the Grateful Dead and others; and Michael Kane, who went on to play bass with Michael Hurley and became a master brewer. His spruce beer was especially esteemed. All three were 20 years old at the time. They were a band.>

< Delusional rant alert...>

If 45-rpm records by Skip James, Bukka White and Son House were released and promoted, Bobby Vinton and Ronnie Dove would be bricked off the set.

<As Gail Collins used to say when she wrote for Long Island Newsday, "One word: hahahahahahahaha.">

Time and *Life* just did articles on rock'n roll. The articles were good, sympathetic, and all things considered, very accurate.

Nothing much happens in Syracuse, but there's a couple of people there. Baltimore and Syracuse both have a lot of good radio stations and are full of interesting objects.

There's plenty of serviceable electric guitars and basses on South Street in Philadelphia. Many basses for between $40 and $100.

Among other people who are very good and mostly unknown, there is Max Oaks, who plays country blues well. As does Sam Firk and Bill Barth.

Peggy Seeger is one of the best banjo players in the world.

Speaking of best in worlds: we saw Joseph Spence when he was in Boston. Spence is undoubtedly one of the finest musicians that mankind has ever known. One way to tell (for myself) if a song is good is if I can't remember any of it immediately after the first few times I hear it.

<This is no longer true for me.>

When we got the Spence record on Elektra, it sounded like a completely different record the first several times I played it. The second time I played it, Weber wanted to know if it was another new Spence record. Spence music is wonderful first thing in the morning.

In 1957, the way I used to get up was to play all my Little Richard records in a row. I had a complete collection, even the ones on Peacock (Little Richard and The Tempo Toppers) and RCA. The Peacock and RCA ones weren't so hot but a couple songs--"Rice, Red Beans, and Turnip Greens" for example--were pretty good.

Volume IV, No. 10 • July 7, 1965

The last time we touched down in New York, Antonia and I went to a Rolling Stone concert. We were lucky to catch it. There was almost no advance publicity. We heard of it on a radio ad the day before it was held.

For one thing, the two music groups that preceded the Rolling Stones were good. The first one especially, a six-member group called the Denims. They did all original material mainly influenced by the English sound and the Beach Boys. They're a Long Island group and very young--mostly between 18 and 21. They just signed a contract with Columbia.

The other group was curious--eight people!--four who played and four who sang and danced very acrobatically. The four who sang had their hair dyed different pastel shades.

They did mostly original stuff. They were called the Visions.

Anyway, among the nasty things people with paunches have been saying about the Beatles and the Stones is that the Beatles and the Stones are ugly and their fans are for the most part, especially Stones fans, are ugly girls. The implication seems to be that the pretty, nice girls like Dean Martin, or the younger, gut-singing, Vitalis squad like Jack Jones or Andy Williams. Anybody who thinks Dean Martin, Jack Jones or Andy Williams are better looking than George Harrison would probably prefer Edgar Guest to E. E. Cummings, and probably drown their steak with ketchup.

<Edgar Guest had a newspaper column, Jus' Folks. A poem a day. Boy, did his poems stink. Sample: Happy Birthday, Happy Birthday, This is what must be a Mirthday. From a poem called, yes!, "Happy Birthday".>

Although the girls who shrieked loudest, longest and soonest were, mostly, the less attractive girls, they were a small minority--about 10% of the crowd. As for the rest of the girls, I have never seen so many good-looking chicks--and what incredible variety--in one place in my life.

The female/male balance was anywhere between 2/3 and 4/5 female, but the males there tended to be a lot more interesting looking than average.

The theatre--the Academy of Music on East 14th Street--was packed and curious odors of diverse kinds wafted about. By the time the Stones were on, the whole audience was on its feet, the entire last several rows standing on top of their seats. The show had to be stopped several times because the aisles were packed with screaming chicks, and no one could get out to go to the john.

A bunch of chicks who had made it backstage charged Charlie Watts, and immediately all kinds of cops (boy, were they fast) rushed in to save him--this in the middle of a song--and the Stones never even stopped playing. It was Charlie's birthday and groups of chicks kept singing "Happy Birthday" to him.

Whenever the show would be stopped, a bunch of chicks in back of us would sing "We Shall Overcome."

One of the disc jockeys who mc'd was called Scott something-or-other (every city has a DJ named Scott something-or-other), and whenever he was on stage, a chick would shriek "Scott rots!"

<That was Scott Muni, I think.>

Whoever it was who arranged the show is lining up more shows with the Kinks, the Zombies and Herman's Hermits.

Concerts are much more fun when everyone is a little bit hysterical.

A couple chicks were ambulanced and one threw up.

Volume IV, No. 11 • July 21, 1965

This is going to be about the evolution behind the so-called hippy uniform, folk variety. Is that clear?

I will only cover the time I was on the set, from 1958. Back then the main influence was Pete Seeger: army shoes, baggy pants, five-pointed star on banjo peghead, etc. The whole thing was a mildly-dated, working-class bit. You know the political cartoon version of WORKINGMAN: broad shoulders, wide grin, Tom Joad hat.

The same year the Kingston Trio arrived. They dressed like young Johns.

<Johns was the name hookers used for their clients.>

That's because some publicist thought that's how college boys looked.

Young John folksingers and coffeehouses quickly joined forces (1959-1961) mainly because coffeehouse owners felt audiences were more secure when young John types were on stage. Ideally, folksingers were supposed to look like a nice date for sis.

Elsewhere people on the set wore cowboy hats, sometimes doing a whole cowboy thing, sometimes with fetishy variations, like white Levis. Bluegrass people sometimes went vaguely cowboyish, too. In 1960, I remember people buying used cowboy hats in Salvation Armies. Stetsons for 50¢.

Boots were as hip then as now; boots are always a hit. Then they were mostly Wellingtons, jodhpurs and, of course, cowboy boots. In 1960, while in New York, I had a pair of black knee-length boots that I wore with pants tucked in. Everyone I knew made it a point to tell me that was the wrong way to wear them. The idea seemed to be: don't let on how far your boots go. Things were more uptight in 1960.

Also cracking in 1958 were the New Lost City Ramblers, who pioneered the old-timey look: vests, square-type shoes, watch chains, mildly archaic hairstyles, etc. And expensive but used-for-decades clothes.

<In the Aughties, I asked John Cohen about this and he said it started when the New Lost City Ramblers had an East Coast college gig, and they weren't allowed on stage unless they wore suits, this is still being the uptight '50s. So they went to a pawn shop, where they all bought pre-World War Two suits.>

By 1962, big city antique stores were selling 1920s dresses which were only moderately expensive. And Steve Weber was pioneering those old-timely, wire, small-lens shades that Roger McGuinn would be wearing three years later. Chicks doing the old-timey thing usually dressed like cats: jeans, blue work shirts, boots, etc. Or, they would go for a peasant-gingham look.

Prior to the Beatnik thing (also 1958), Bohemian types were wearing work clothes, but they were always immaculate. However, the sloppy loser look replaced it. This started to turn around with the advent of the Beatles in 1964. The whole loser syndrome, which was perhaps the most disgusting aspect of folk music, was overwhelmed. Since the Beatles came along, all the professional failures, who said it was impossible to be good and sell at the same time, have been answered finally.

The folk hippy fetish costume before the Beatles was usually loser-drag. Since the Beatles, this has been changing. After all, who really wants to look like a junkie?

Then there's the rocker-leather-motorcycle look. Leather is necessary if you're on a motorcycle because it may save your life or a half-inch of flesh. The rocker costume is a motorcycle costume. Motorcycle costumes are a gas. The motorcycle look for nonmotorcyclists is going to be very big in two years.

In short, it has become fashionable to look your best rather than your worst. I think this is very healthy. A massive synthesis between old-timey, California casual, contemporary English-Bohemian and diverse fetish-wear is on the horizon. Even metal fetishism is a coming thing.

Anyway, I think it's all loads of fun and *Harper's Bazaar* is one of my favorite magazines.

Volume IV, No. 12 <*Antonia wrote this one, by herself*> • **August 4, 1965**

Back when the human race was an unlikely runt, our forefathers had to devote their day to searching for the fruits, berries, and grubs (which formed the basis of their diet because grubs were not very large, as animals, and had few means of self-defense).

Man's only advantage was a superior brain, but there was one drawback: with all the time it took to gather food, there was no time to eat. Destruction loomed imminent unless an easily harvested source of food energy could be found. One day, someone hit on it. MEAT! A meat meal would keep you running, so man became carnivorous.

He hunted in packs. His chances were good in groups and man was gregarious anyway. After a kill, the hunters would sit around, re-enacting their part in the hunt and trying to outdo the other. Some storytelling worked better than others and these would be repeated. After a while, listeners would know what was coming and would sometimes join in with the words. This, roughly, was the beginning of music as entertainment.

Rhythm happened. The participants added effectiveness and drama by knocking together sticks, stones, or anything handy. The culture grew; the drum was invented. Hunting songs and dances became formalized and recognizable music was on its way.

Now let us flash forward to the modern world. Music is everywhere. It has been plugged in, piped in, and tuned in to every conceivable part of our lives. But one thing is in notably short supply. It is that hard-bop, forward-driving whooping, bloodthirsty basic quality that sent the puny cavemen off courageously to hunt mammoths. Modern songs often whine, complain, drool, wallow and generally go on about what a rotten world we're living in, and what a hard road we're travelling, and how love has put us down so we can't go on living. With singers to match. This stuff is depressing and just plain boring, but at least it's SAFE. People hear it and are reassured; we are all civilized. The weak can survive as well as the strong now. Indeed, they are inheriting the earth, and very few people want to listen to music that reminds them of our nasty carnivore past.

There is a ray of hope. The kids, fed to upchucking with cotton candy and plastic orgasms, are casting about in search of something real. The strong, old virtues such as honor, self-respect, and justice are making a comeback. And the kind of music these kids like and often play is the strong, simple gutgrabbing kind that makes you jump up and down and whoop with joy that you were born human. In short, music to Eat Meat By. Crude? Vulgar? Sure! But along the way, the more modern sense of melody and "prettyness" has mixed in. At its best, modern, popular music can reach the intellects, souls, hearts, and balls of its listeners. It's the most broad-beamed sound ever produced, and it's become the solid foundation of something real: a time when survival was perilous and a man had to have great confidence in his own power to even stick his nose out of the cave. What cave, I wonder, are these kids getting ready to walk out of? The black hole of contempt for human nature their culture has put them in? It looks that way to me. They are unarmed and lack experience, but they've still got that old stand-by, the human brain. That may be all they need. The last mammoth died a long time ago. Happy hunting.

Volume IV, No. 13 • August 18, 1965

<In which my anxiety about the Rounders falling apart begins to manifest...>

Something cancerous has been groping the planet since May. As Charley Patten said, "Evil, evil all around."

Popular music is an always-boss barometer of collective changes of Universal Soul. The popular musicians who have the most complete grasp on reality (are in tune with the beat of the universe) (swinging with the cosmos) are the most accurate barometers. So since May, the Rolling Stones "Can't get no satisfaction", while the Beatles holler, "Help!", the Supremes sing, "Nothing but heartaches" while Dylan asks, "How does it feel?"

The stock market has been going down since May 1st.

During May, June and July, there's been a spate of garbage records--like Presley "Crying in the Chapel". Presley died in 1958.

The rot that's been happening is the death spasm of all the old creeps who refuse "to get out of the road if you can't lend a hand cause the times they are a-changing". All those creeps, however, are dead. The old fools are as out of date as the dinosaur. When those old creeps die, there will be no one to replace them--all the segregation creeps, for instance. When they are dead, and they're already paunchy and balding, segregation will be as dead as Nazi Germany.

Old saw: "Let the dead bury the dead."

<56 years later, dream on, kid.>

On to other things. There's a Marshall McLuhan book called *Understanding Media: The Extensions of Man.* There's a McGraw-Hill paperback edition out that sells for $1.95. The book explains exactly what is happening to the world and why. Briefly, the whole planet is re-organizing on a tribal basis.

The reason for this is electronics. Electronics connect; the pre-electronic scene was mechanical. Mechanical = separation, specialization. Electric = connection. The preface of the book said many things I've known unconsciously but never realized. I've been reading the book and saying, "Of course!", "Oh, yeah!", "Sure", "Oh, that's why!", etc. Read it! Read it! You will be in a much better position to deal with now, and if you don't deal with now, now will deal with you. Take your pick.

We just saw the Butterfield Band and the Chambers Brothers for the first time. Lead guitar player for the Butterfield Band is a total ace. But that drummer, Sam Lay! Absolutely one of the finest drummers on the planet.

The Chambers Brothers have a sound I haven't heard any R&B group have in a long time. I've been starving for that sound. Listening to them put me in a state of pure glory. Both the Butterfield Band and the Chambers Brothers were working at the Au Go Go in New York. Barbara Dane did a set, too. I had never heard her sing although I've been hearing about her since the late '50s. She is fine! What a joy to see a woman in these girl-oriented times. The ideal dream girl used to be 18. She is now 14. I mean the average adult male's ideal dream girl. The fact that 14-year olds are aware of this is one of the things that makes now so strange. A pendulum swing is coming and women are going to be popular again.

I heard Kathy & Carol for the first time. They are light years ahead of any girl duo I have ever heard anywhere. Endless multilevel blessings on them! Buy their record and you will help the whole human race.

Two days ago, I heard Dayle Stanley's record *After the Snow*. I have not been so amazed and delighted by any record of a girl folksinger since I heard Peggy Seeger for the first time in 1958. I have never liked trained voices in women. I love Dayle's voice. Her guitar playing is superb and flawless. The words, too. Some are hers, some are her husband's, some are from friends. They are all real words saying real things. The power of her voice is awe-inspiring. She has so incredibly much to offer the world. Long live Dayle Stanley! Buy her records! Make them a part of your life. They already are if you've got a life worthy of the name.

<Her song, "The Years", that she wrote when was 13, is my 1964 song of my 100. I was unable to find when she was born for my liner notes, nor her whereabouts. I was told she has dementia.>

If you haven't seen *What's New Pussycat?*, see it. It's a Yippee movie!

Volume IV, No. 17 • October 13, 1965

A while ago, I said I wouldn't mention any lousy people because they would crash in various ways anyway, but I feel the need to spread some venom, so I'll just make a big list of CREEPS who are taking up SPACE that many other people could fill MUCH BETTER.

<Some of these people I no longer consider to be creeps. Rather than explain why I thought they were, I will simply label them (retract). This list could have been a lot longer.>

List of creeps:

Ronnie Dove (possibly the most annoying of all manufactured teen idols ever, and thankfully largely forgotten)
Bobby Vinton (retract)
Bobby Darin (retract)
Bobby Rydell (retract)
Charles de Gaulle
Connie Francis (retract)
J. Edgar Hoover
Joey Heatherton (retract)
Sandra Dee (retract)
Trini Lopez (retract)
Johnny Rivers (retract)
Dave Clark 5 (retract)
Paul Anka (still here because of his awful song, "You're Having My Baby")
Arthur Prysock (retract)
Gene Pitney (retract, retract, what was I thinking?)
Dean Martin (retract)
Frank Sinatra (retract)
Doris Day (retract)
Ernest Hemingway (retract)
F. Scott Fitzgerald (retract)
Kahlil Gibran
Sonny & Cher (retract Cher, not Sonny)
Serendipity Singers (who cares? retract)
Jody Miller (don't remember anything about her)
Robert Goulet (retract)
Elvis Presley (retract)
Al Hirt (retract, kinda)
Jay & the Americans (retract)
Patti Page (aw, Patti! retract)
Ezra Pound (anti-Semites are still creeps)

AHHH! I feel BETTER. Ain't nothing like throwing rocks at dogs when you 're feeling down.

Now I'll tell about some good things.

The record by THEM on the Parrot label.

<Van Morrison's first.>

A fine fat LP stuffed full of incredible jelly! A licking good hit! Play it full blast and give all your creep neighbors a headache. Banzai!

The two-record set by *The Miracles: Greatest Hits from the Beginning*. Lead singer Smokey Robinson wrote and arranged most or all of them. He is one of the finest singers going. Incredible range, subtlety and taste. Modern classic! Tamla Records.

All Day Singing From The Sacred Harp. Southern Journey, Volume 7. This was reviewed by BROADSIDE a little while ago, but I just bought it and play it a lot. Invaluable to learn harmony from, and to get up in the morning by. STRANGE music that people sometimes have to adjust to, but it's TRUE PRIMAL FOLK JUICE, and you better get used to it or burn your guitar and make a good act of contrition. Prestige International. (Sacred harp singing is early American folk: PURE GLORY a cappella holy noise.)

The Yardbirds have a record out on Epic. They are good now and getting better. Whole record original except for a couple ("My Girl Sloopy" and "Hey Little School Girl") and those are done in totally new way. Very good liner notes, funny as hell but not long enough.

If you haven't heard the *Out of Our Heads* record by the Stones, what are you, a dope? Stands at the pinnacle of contemporary cultural achievement and flaps! A beacon brightly shining in the vague firmament.

Help!, is a good, funny, see-it flick.

Cat Ballou, stunk on ice.

Harlow is a whoop! Carol Baker is an incredibly bad actress but a first-rate, accidentally funny lady. Flick ends with color stills of Harlow by Baker while Bobby Vinton sings "Lonely Girl." PERFECT!

Bunch of current paperbound grist:

Sometimes a Great Notion, by Ken Kesey, who wrote One Flew Over the Cuckoo's Nest. This is his second novel and even better. Kesey is one of the best writers we have, some others being Theodore Sturgeon, Terry Southern and Philip K. Dick.

<Philip K. Dick was first published by my father-in-law-to-be, Donald A. Wollheim.>

I Never Promised You a Rose Garden, by Hannah Greene. Signet Books. This might be hard to find. It came out last March. It's about a 16-year old girl who's very smart and crazy since childhood, and how she stops being crazy. The book is well written, etc., but what impressed me most was the fact that I have never seen a more accurate depiction of insanity. What a good job.

Only Lovers Left Alive, by Dave Wallis. All the adults have committed suicide and the teenagers take over. And it's well done. Bantam Books.

Keep your hand on the plow, hold on.

Volume IV, No. 20 • November 24, 1965

By now the Lovin' Spoonful album has been out and released for a couple of weeks. Two of my favorites are "Younger Girl" and "Did You Ever Have to Make Up Your Mind?" which are recent Sebastian tunes. *<About the Baez sisters, Joan and Mimi.>* John is getting fantastic. The Spoonful is getting fantastic. Just what we need! Silly Heroes!

And there is a new group (new to me, they have been together for over a year) called the Charlatans. People have been talking about "the next thing" in popular music. The next thing, in my opinion, is a mixture of rhythm and blues, Stones' variety, old-timey country blues, and African-style rhythm patterns, that is, each instrument often keeping a different but synchronized beat than the others. Anyway, that's the Charlatans. Their sound is one of the greatest things I've ever heard in my life. They're from Berkeley/San Francisco; there are five of them; they have been doing mostly traditional tunes and now are writing their own songs. They look like English rock-type hippy cowboys. Some sing rock style, some sing mountain style. There's been much bilge about folk-rock this year. Most touted folk-rock groups don't folk and can't rock. The Turtles, for example. *<Oh, come on Stampfel—the Turtles aren't folk rock and they're okay.>*

All these little kids trying to be Bob Dylan. They should try someone easy, like King Arthur! How could any of them hope to do a better job at being Dylan than Dylan can?

Folk-rock is now where folk music was in 1958–62. What happened to folk music in 1962 was, in simple terms: Dylan, John Hurt and Doc Watson. The Kingston Trio, etc., haven't been anything to worry about since. The Turtles, Sonny & Cher, etc., are to folk-rock as the Kingston Trio and The Brothers Four, etc., are to folk music. And Dylan––who was playing rock piano for Bobby Vee and Gene Vincent before he ever heard of folk music––the Spoonful and the Charlatans are examples of "real" folk rock.

No record is currently out by the Charlatans. One is being worked on. You won't have to wait too long.

Just heard the new Yardbirds 45: "I'm A Man." Wow! In my last column, I touted the Yardbirds LP, which I've had a chance to hear a lot more. The more I hear it, the better I like it. There is not a bad or so-so cut on the record. And they seemed ready to take a big musical jump, comparable to the one the Stones made with "This Will Be the Last Time" and "Satisfaction". "Get Off My Cloud" is, incidentally, great, but I like the other side, "I'm Free", even better.

The Yardbirds have been very big in England for a long time. Most of this time, they were an in-group thing, like Dylan was here. I quiver and drool in anticipation for their next LP.

The two-record set, *The Miracles: Greatest Hits From the Beginning* that I mentioned last column is another thing I have been listening to with increasing pleasure. Most of the cuts are "A", the rest are "B." And the Miracles' "B" is as good as most people's "A".

Nice paperbacks. *Dr. Bloodmoney, or How We Got Along After the Bomb*, by Philip K. Dick. Ace Books, published this year. 40¢. Lots of interesting stuff about mutants, like an intelligent, hairless rat that plays nose flute. Very, very well done characters, who grow and change. The plot surprised the hell out of me, which usually doesn't happen.

<Again, this book was bought and edited by Donald A. Wollheim, my future father-in-law.>

There's all these groovy writers around all of a sudden. Most of them appeared simultaneously with all those groovy musicians who have cracked since 1962. Terry Southern; the Beatles; Philip K. Dick; Dylan; Ken Kesey; the Stones; Kurt Vonnegut, Jr.; The Kweskin Jug Band; Joseph Heller; John Fahey; Tom Wolfe; Them, etc., etc. Jelly, jelly, jelly!

Volume IV, No. 21 • December 8, 1965

<Some of you may have noticed that my writing has been profoundly influenced by Ed Sanders, as is evident below. Incidentally, two of my other main writing influences have been Harvey Kurtzman and Tom Wolfe.>

Alert! Alert! We are under attack by SLIME MONSTERS! PUKE DEMONS! PHLEGMINADE PEDDLERS! There's all this crap music on the radio. Since May. Stop the swine! Stop them!

HERE IS A LIST. IT IS A MAGIC LIST. HERE IS HOW IT WORKS.

BUY one of these. INSTANTLY, you zap all the other ones on the list. There is a vast POWER LINK-UP. Freak Beams instantly zap all creeps everywhere. Give them MIGRAINES, ULCERS, HEART ATTACKS! YIPPEE!

Here are records with not one bad cut on them! Pure glory! INEFFABLE jelly! Slurp city!

The Rolling Stones, *12 x 5*
The Rolling Stones, *The Rolling Stones Now*
The Rolling Stones, *Out of Our Heads*
The Beatles, (There are about 7 cuts of theirs ever that I haven't liked; about 70 that I've loved.) *<Decades later, in retrospect, maybe 3.>*
The Miracles, *The Miracles Greatest Hits From the Beginning*

Kathy & Carol, *Kathy & Carol*
Jimmy Reed, *I'm Jimmy Reed*

(I've never heard him do a bad or dull thing.)

The Four Seasons, *Golden Hits of the Four Seasons*
Joseph Spence, *Happy All the Time*
Joseph Spence, *Bahamian Folk*
Music Mountain Music of Kentucky
Ewan MacColl & A. L. Lloyd, *Thar She Blows!*
The Harry Smith Anthology (All six records. Really!)
The Mississippi Blues: 1927 to 1941
The Holy Modal Rounders
The Yardbirds, *For Your Love*

(Watch for their new one! I've heard it's beyond belief.)

Them, *Here Comes the Night*
Dayle Stanley, *After the Snow*
Bob Dylan, *Bob Dylan, Another Side of Bob Dylan, The Freewheelin' Bob Dylan, Bringing it all Back Home, Highway 61 Revisited*

Jim Kweskin & the Jug Band (Their second album. I never heard their first one.)

(I need more money for records! I gotta get some kind of scene where I can hustle free records...on! on!)

Fred MacDoweil, *The Delta Blues*
Bukka White, *Sky Songs, etc.*
John Fahey, *Death Chants, Breakdowns & Military Waltzes*
Original Sound Track, *What's New Pussycat?*
The Lovin' Spoonful, *Do You Believe in Magic?*
Little Richard, *Here's Little Richard*

There are many others I would list, but I never heard a whole LP of theirs. Notably, the Kinks, the Zombies, Otis Redding, the Beach Boys, etc.

There is a game I invented called "Soup". All you need are IN-CREDIBLE 45-rpm records. INCREDIBLE 45s are records that stand as milestones along the rocky road of cultural progress in a changing world and perform countless actions. The way you play is take five, six, seven or however many records will play at once, and play them over and over! Loud! It's very uplifting and fun, too.

Here is a sample list of some of the all-time incredible records of history!

"Love Is Strange" - Mickey & Sylvia
"Summertime Summertime" - The Jamies
"Surfer Bird" - The Trashmen
"Louie Louie" - Richard Berry
"Fun Fun Fun" - Beach Boys
"Be My Baby" - The Ronnettes
"Heat Wave" - Martha & the Vandellas

Most of the recordings of the Beatles, Stones, Miracles, Otis Redding, Yardbirds, Them

"Long Tall Sally" – Little Richard
"Slippin' & Slidin'" – Little Richard
"Tutti Frutti" – Little Richard
"Lucille" – Little Richard
"I'm In Love Again" – Fats Domino
"Whole Lotta Shakin' Goin' On" – Jerry Lee Lewis
"He's A Rebel" – The Crystals
"He Is So Fine" – The Chiffons
"Come & Get These Memories" – Martha & the Vandellas
"Sally Go 'Round the Roses" – The Jaynettes
"Anyone Who Had a Heart" – Dionne Warwick
"The Way You Do the Things You Do" – The Temptations
"The Shoop Shoop Song" – Betty Euntt
"The Nitty Gritty" – Shirley Ellis
"Peggy Sue" – Buddy Holly
"Bye Bye Love" – The Everly Brothers
"I Wonder If I Care As Much" – The Everly Brothers

I'll continue that list later; it's part of my life's work.

Volume IV, No. 22 <Written by Antonia> • **December 22, 1965**

Since magic has been an increasingly popular subject for speculation, I decided to sort it all out and see what made sense. First of all,
it seems to exist. At least there are things science can't explain yet, so
they put them under the heading of magic.

Magic comes in two kinds: black and white. Black magic is intended to do evil and white magic to do good. That sounds like a very
simple line of division. Actually, it's not.

The first thing to remember is magic is circular. That is, it always
comes back to the magician. If you do good, you become good and
good is attracted to you (or vice versa). However, the "good" or "bad"
results of magic are not simply the ends you want to achieve, but the
sum total of all the changes resulting from your magic. Of course
we can't know all the results of everything we do. But if we choose

to deal with magic, we must be careful to take as many factors into account as we can beforehand. Remember, the results come back on the magician's head. Irresponsibility can be disastrous. When we deal with magic, we are dealing with forces we don't completely understand. Therefore, it seems best to treat it with respect and not use it casually for every little thing that comes along. You never know what might get out of whack. If there's some non-magical solution to your problem, try that first. Your magic will be all the better for it.

There is no rigid formula for spells. The spells that have been handed down to us are things that have worked for certain people. If they "feel" right to you, they may work for you, too. If not, invent your own. Always trust your intuition when making up a spell. The subconscious understands magic better than the conscious mind. Something to focus your attention on helps. If you've got pictures, music, or small objects that remind you of the spell you're trying to cast, use them. Some magic is best done by one person, some by two, etc. Generally speaking, major changes require a man and a woman. Also, it's best not to have more than one confidant.

Now we come to a popular subject, namely, curses. Just about everyone who's thought about doing magic has thought about getting back at someone who did them wrong; blighting their crops for seven years, etc. WATCH OUT! Remember the magic's going to come back on you. If your enemy is a person who is genuinely doing evil in the world, stopping him is "White Magic". But if he's just someone who's bugging you, forget about the magic. Punch him out or send him a cowflop in the mail.

All in all, magic requires patience. Long-range, carefully worked out spells seem to be the best. And there is no spell that can save you from the consequences of your own actions. After all, you're still dealing with the real world. I'm sorry if all this sounds overcautious, I'm really not trying to take all the fun out of magic. It's just that there's a lot I don't understand. And I'd rather not fly any blinder than I have to.

1966 as THE VEER CITY RIDER

Volume IV, No. 23 • January 5, 1966

In my recent lists of good things, one name that came up frequently was The Rolling Stones. Today instead of simply hollering, "Hooray for The Rolling Stones," again I'll try to figure out why. So if you have no use for The Stones, or don't want one, tune me out now.

What are The Rolling Stones, anyway? Five young English cats who play sort of rhythm and blues and write a lot of their own stuff. Well, that's not so unusual.

They can play music. That is, they can all find their way around their instruments. This is standard for modern rock and roll groups. The Stones also know how to work in terms of each other. They play together without stepping on each other's feet. That's a little less usual. And Keith Richard, the lead guitarist, has some pretty funny ideas about putting guitar noises together—pretty off-the-wall harmony ideas too. He's also half of the songwriting team.

The other songwriter is Mick Jagger. He's also the lead singer. He sings a hell of a lot like Mick Jagger and people usually don't like it at first. The first thing you might notice is his sense of timing, which is as good as any actor's you would care to name. "But," you say, listening again, "this guy can't be serious." He ain't.

None of them are. They find the world funny, people's ideas about them funnier yet, and the whole business of being The Rolling Stones excruciatingly hilarious. They're just about completely irreverent.

This approach runs through everything they do. With their scruffy clothes and outspoken comments, they have taken the traditional adolescent-hero position of "rebel" and "non-conformist". But they can't keep a straight face through it all. "We can't comb our hair," one Stone tells reporters, "It'll mess up our public image." All this suggesting that social conscience is no excuse for martyrdom. The ultimate silliness, it seems, is crying about being born into a world you never made. If you don't like it, change it, but, for crissake, stop whimpering.

This attitude becomes more obvious in their recent songs. They seem determined to prove you can get away with anything as long as you stay on top of it. Their stage appearances are unbelievable. The four instrumental Stones stand in an almost stationary line across the stage while playing--Jagger moves enough for five, dancing, wiggling, mugging, swishing and making nasty faces. The first time I saw him I thought he kept going back and forth between looking like the last Neanderthal and the first Cro-Magnon.

The Stones have a fine-tuning control over the audience. If things get dull they'll incite a riot. The audience feels very personally connected with The Stones. The young girls find them sexy. The Stones find this pretty hilarious, too. That's the main thing, I guess--their attitude. The trouble with most social protest is that it's such a drag. The Stones are showing us that you can use your head without losing your sense of humor.

<Brian Jones actually started the group and named the group, and was responsible for the best hooks in numerous songs. I wasn't aware of that when I wrote this column.>

Volume IV, No. 24 • January 19, 1966

A cure! A cure! The tides of phlegm are lurching back to OBLIVION! HAPPY NEW YEAR!

I'm writing this, incidentally, 1 January 1966. It's 60 degrees and there's no subways or buses, but we got a mayor with hair and things could be worse.

What a December! Our bathroom ceiling fell and water dripped down from at least a dozen places and we had to hold an umbrella over our heads when we used the throne. Cold, used water dripped.

Total bringdown. Our slimelord, Malek, inspired this song over a year ago.

Who is our landlord?
Moise Malek!
Moise Malek!
(pronounced moy-sha mah-lik).
Who is our landlord?
Moise Malek!
Moise Malek!
If he don't do what you said, hit him
in the head!
If he don't do what you said again, hit him
in the head again!
Moise Malek!
Moise Malek!

Anyway, the slime creep can't be found and besides somebody broke our door down and the whole area inside the door of the apartment house--that rotting hulk--is a hangout for young kids (some are nice, some are creepy) who write incredible things on the wall, like--just a second, I'll go out and look--I just went out and it smelled of urine, so I came back in.

Anyway, people write things like "Big Bad Dodge", "True love never dies" and "No beatniks, n------, sp---, etc. allowed in this building; only IRISH CIVILIZED WHITES!" Wow.

Anyway, a cure! The slime on the pop stations was bringing us down, so we started listening to WNJR and WWRL (1420 and 1590, New Jersey and New York) more again, and was amazed at the records out! Rhythm & Blues is blowing total high renaissance! Here are 10 current records that are as good as anything ever done:

"This Can't Be True", Eddy Holmon
"Let's Do The Boston Monkey", Les Couper and The Soul Rockers
"Are You There", Dionne Warwick

"Recovery", Fontella Bass
"Just One More Day", Otis Redding
"He's A Most Unusual Boy", Patti Austin
"Hurts So Bad", Willie Bobo
"Flashback", The Soul Sisters
"You Blow My Mind", Hugh McCracklin
"All Or Nothing", Patti LaBelle and The Blue Belles

Some of those names might be misspelled, but there's 10 classics, not to mention all the plenty-good-enough records. About 70–90% of the records on rhythm & blues stations are listenable. Barely half the records on pop stations are listenable, although as late as last May, 80% were listenable listenableistenableistenable!

"You get yours--I got mine, it's monkey time", from "Monkey Time", Major Lance, Summer 1963.

So once in a while we turn on pop and hear "Well-Respected Man", which I'm hung on, and "Michelle" and we turn on R&B again.

Wow, Summer 1963! "Heat Wave", "Be My Baby", "Sally Go Round The Roses", anyway, rhythm & blues is going to crack SO BIG this year. Hard Bop! That is the essence of the 1966 change. For instance, The Yardbirds are now in the same class as The Beatles and The Stones. The LP Rave *Up With The Yardbirds* is beyond belief! What a good record! Buy it and writhe! Also *Otis Blue* by Otis Redding. Otis Redding is one of the consummate artists of all time, his singing, songwriting, arranging--I just play the record over and over and lie on the bed on my back with my mouth open.

Also Patti LaBelle and The Blue Belles! Patti is one of the best singers around. They were on the same show as The Stones in Philadelphia that we saw and all the chicks in the group took turn singing lead and they were all great. We just got a Patti LaBelle record about two years old, and it knocked us out. You know that "Water" song: "Each day I face the burning waste without taste of water, cool, clear water"? They do the best version of it I ever heard. Also, the best version of

"When Johnny Comes Marching Home Again", besides all their regular great stuff. But Patti's incredible, multi-octave, multi-level singing-- it's the other side of what Dionne Warwick sings. And Patti does her thing as good as Dionne does hers. I believe they're both from South Philadelphia which is a hard bop place if there ever was one.

Don't miss the boat.

Volume IV, No. 25 • February 2, 1966

As long as I can remember, I've been interested in different scenes and how and why they work, for example, the motorcycle scene, the folk music scene, the political scene, etc. All scenes tend to split into factions, splinter groups, etc. You get more than two people and you got a scene, and three people are almost always divided two against one, with the two and one constantly switching places. I think of my scene-digging as "sociology".

Last summer Antonia and I got interested in the teenage fads scene. Ever since, we've been buying all the teenage magazines and looking at them, and Antonia's been cutting pictures out of them and putting them up in our john, mainly Beatles, Stones and Yardbirds. Then came the catastrophic flood from the mad, paranoid Chinese cat upstairs. When we'd pound on his door to tell him quit splashing, his eye would appear in his peekhole and he'd holler "no spic English, no spic English" and run away. To this day we've never seen him and think maybe he's a floating cloud with an eye in it, 'cause all we ever saw was his eye.

So the water came down--tepid, murky, acrid, sallow water. As winter came, the water grew colder. Still the water came down, and all the pictures turned brown and worse. But finally the landlord fixed it and we put up shocking pink burlap and a velvet pink draw-cord with rhinestones on it to turn on the light and we're gonna put up sequins and gold and silver stuff and more pictures, mostly of the Stones. Can't beat a happy ending.

Back to the teenage magazines. Most of them are put out by money-grabbing creeps who are stupid and should be destroyed for eugenic reasons--or at least spayed. But there are a couple of good ones, the best of the lot being *Rave*, which is English and costs 50¢ here. The Rave people are smart, have self-respect and respect the people who buy their magazine. It's printed on good shiny paper and has lots of excellent color photographs, the best of any music mag, and many two-page spreads. They tell how to copy expensive clothes for cheap. No other teenage mag I know does this. Real groovy ideas, like take a fancy slip or nightgown, attach ribbons, sequins, etc. and you've got a discotheque dress to carry on in. This is useful for young chicks, especially English ones, who have less bread.

Music Echo is printed on newsprint and, again, is English. It has pictures, lists of pop songs, articles, and columns. Its record review-ers are mostly stupid and tasteless, and it used to have a column by Andrew Loog Oldham, who manages the Stones. I liked his column; I didn't always agree with him, but it was a fun read. His column was discontinued because of adverse mail after he criticized people like Sonny and Cher. Now they got Jonathan King doing a column and he's a pretentious ass, but *Music Echo* always gives you your money's worth of useful information. There's a lot of good inside stuff like who did what on records I've been wondering about, for instance.

The only other ones we've seen that are any good are *Teen Screen*, *16* and *Fabulous*. The first two are American; the last, English. These magazines tout a lot of people who should be dipped in phlegm and allowed to harden, but they don't do what every other teenage mag-azine we've seen so far does--consider their reader as being nine or ten years old and very stupid.

I've always liked the magazines with the words to songs in them. *Hit Parader* and *Song Hits* are two that have a lot of good articles and background material, but they pre-date the teenage magazine thing, which started as far as I know with *Dig* magazine in 1956.

Corn flakes and blueberries and corn flakes and peaches are very good, too.

More shards. First concerning our recently released Prestige record. It was cut in mid-1964; it took them only a year and a half to get it out. The recording job was done by Sam Charters, whose recording technique sucks rotten eggs. He's a gross butcher. In our first record, I put him up tight so he recorded Weber louder. In this one, Weber put him up tight so he recorded me louder. And Weber was quiet in front. Weber was about at his worst during that session. And--that incredible Prestige touch--the songs are put in the dullest conceivable order. Not only are all the fiddle tunes in a row, but most cuts are in order according to key. In one place, I believe there are 4 cuts in a row in the key of A, and all the cuts with banjo are in a row.

However, this record is not pressed on compressed buffalo dung like the first one. Many people complained that after many playings, our first record wore out and they couldn't hear it any more. It was pressed on a special shoddy disc that was 30¢ cheaper than the regular one. Despite all these drawbacks, us at our worst are better than 95% of the people in folk music at their best. Several people have even told me this record sounds better than our first one. The liner notes are good, too. Buy it. In 5 years, it'll be a collector's item. *<55 years later, it's still in print.>*

Incidentally, Phil Spiro said something about the fact that we always play things the same way. We always played them different. We never did a song the same way twice. Ever. No complaint about Phil, he does the best and most tasteful reviews in BROADSIDE.

Now, the Fugs record. I just heard it for the first time a week ago. I'm just on two cuts: "Swinburne Stomp" and "Nothing". I quit playing with them when I quit playing with Weber. The record sounds a lot better than I thought it would, and when I talked to Ken Weaver, their drummer, a week ago, he said they play worlds better than the record. Best thing on the record is the incredible Weber tune, "Boobs a Lot". Weber was, incidentally, kicked out of the Fugs in January for irresponsibility. The band waited for him almost an hour before going on, and when they finally went to see what was going on, he had fallen asleep in a box. Aiee! The cut of "Nothing" is where Harry Smith (of Anthology fame), the producer, broke a wine bottle in the middle. Listen really hard. *<I think Sanders said it was a rum bottle, during the recording of "Swinburne Stomp".>*

Just saw the new *Hit Parader*. It has a page about the CHARLA-TANS, who I hosanned a few issues ago. You can look at them now! Buy it and see!

The Stones put out their own magazine in England. It's called *The Rolling Stones Book*, and it's a slick black-and-white monthly, and it's great. It costs $4 per year in America and is worth each penny. Address:

The Rolling Stones Book,
Beat Publications Ltd.
36-38 Westbourne Grove
London W2, England

Lastly, the reason for the change in the column head is since Rounders are defunct, I don't want to use that name anymore. Veer City Rider is a pun on a Milwaukee motorcycle gang from the '50s called The Beer City Riders. They drove Harley-Davidsons, which are made in Milwaukee.

Ratios: The Dave Clark 5 are to the Beatles as the Animals are to the Stones as Herb Alpert is to Tito Puente as Joan Baez is to Dayle Stanley as Al Hirt is to Miles Davis.

Volume V, No. 3 • March 30, 1966

Last December we were feeling exceptionally nasty. While nasty, we thought of nasty things to do to creeps. Worse and worse things we thought of. Finally we thought of the New Jersey phlegm vats to put creeps in. Vast vats of phlegm, 14 feet deep and heated to 120 degrees. The top of the vat is covered with a network of catwalks on which leopards bopped around to make sure no one got out successfully. And all the creeps in it would be trying to crawl up each other all the time. Ha, ha, we snickered. For hippy creeps, like Dave Clark, there would be cool phlegm vats, identical with the others, but maintained at a temperature of 55 degrees. And do you know what? The more we talked about the vats and making people go "splat" into them, the better we felt. Furthermore, whenever we feel nasty ever since we just think of, for instance, Lou Christy and Nancy Sinatra going SPLAT into the cool vat and the nasty-feeling feeling is replaced by a feeling of Deep Satisfaction. We have found the vats, indeed, a PHYSIC BOON!

<I had an attitude about Lou Christy because I loved his first hits, "Two Faces Have I" and "The Gypsy Cried", and hated his new sound in "Lightning Strikes", and I hated "These Boots Are Made For Walking". But Nancy went on to make a number of great tracks with Lee Hazelwood.>

Lightning strikes, "These Boots Are Made For Walking", "Up Tight" and "My Love" BLEECCHH! SPLAT!

<"Up Tight": Yes, the Stevie Wonder song. Hated that one because of the misuse of the hippy phrase, "up tight", which didn't mean all right and out of sight; it meant tense and nervous. And "My Love", Petula Clark: My love is deeper than the deepest ocean, wider than the sky, etc. When it came on Antonia and I would sing along, substituting "cunt" for "love".>

In the meantime, records like Dionne Warwick's "Are You There" weren't played because they were busy with Nancy Sinatra and Pet Clark. The people responsible for this are the program directors. If Noah were a program director, he'd throw out the horses to make room for the warthogs.

For another thing, it is very perceptive of the DJs to play both sides of Beatle records as a matter of course. And it took them only two years to learn! All the ace groups do two-sided hits as a matter of course. Why don't they play the Stones "B" sides? or the Miracles? or the Yardbirds? or the Kinks? or Otis Redding's?

Disc Jockeys. There are some good ones. Almost any rhythm & blues jockey is all right. Almost any pop jockey is a creep. Among hookers, disc jockeys are the lowest. "Anybody want a dj? I told him I'm sick."

<We were hanging out with a number of cool hookers back then. One used to answer the phone with: "House of Pain. Satana speaking." Groupies hadn't quite arrived on the scene yet, but many of the hip hookers were proto-groupies. Or vice-versa.>

It's hard to say which way DJs are most offensive, when they play an awful record and gush, "It's beautiful! It's beautiful! I love it!" Or when they blab over the beginnings and ends of records with especially quiet or subtle beginnings and ends. Let me count the ways.

A few weeks ago we saw Patti LaBelle and the Blue Belles at the Apollo. They're the best chick group I've ever seen. Rhythm & Blues shows are different from pop shows just like R&B radio is different from pop radio--no hysteria and you can hear and see everything that's going on.

Both Sam & Dave and Sam & Bill are several times as good as the Righteous Brothers.

The new Spoonful album is incredible. All the cuts on it but one are their own songs. Their sound is getting more and more like nobody else at all.

There's a Bay Area group called Jefferson Airplane. I haven't heard them yet. They're supposed to be more like the CHARLATANS than anyone else.

<The Airplane got their name from Jorma Kaukonen, by way of Steve Talbott, my first roommate when I moved to Berkeley in 1960. Talbott nicknamed Kaukonen, "Blind Thomas Jefferson Airplane".>

I worked with the Jesse Colin Young–Jerry Corbitt group at the Gaslight for two weeks. They've really taken off since trimmed down to four members. The more I watched them the more I liked them. Usually two weeks of someone else's music is enough to put you up a wall. But more and more of their tunes got through to me. And they kept trying new things every night. Their interest was contagious. By the last week they were getting encores after every set.

David Blue did a few guest sets. He is easily one of the best song-writer musicians in the world.

Volume V, No. 4 • April 10, 1966

All my life I've been hung up on media. All forms. You know, communication.

There was a Batman song I only heard one day, by the Camps. Do you know about the trickle-down theory? I'll explain that later. Anyway, this Batman song had this very chorus:

"We're behind the wheel
of the Batmobile
It's fun-fun-fun to drive in every day."

Really stupid but really funny.

But those nerds at the National Comics group squashed the record along with all "unauthorized" Batman grist.

For a long time (Wow! I just thought back and it goes back to before I could read) I've been hung up on magazines. I've always read several dozen at least every month. Some because I like them, some to see what *those* people were like, most for both reasons and many others too. Here, for instance, is a partial list of the magazines I read every issue of, or only miss once in a great while or when flat broke. I will start with the magazines now in touching distance. I'm writing this on the March '66 *Glamour*. *<I read all the women's magazines Antonia bought.>*

Village Voice
East Village Echo
Time
Teen Screen
Tiger Beat
Teen Life
Harper's Bazaar
Mademoiselle
Playboy
Air Progress
Popular Science
Rave
Fabulous
Billboard (I read other people's)
Cash Box (Going to subscribe)
Fantasy & Science Fiction
BROADSIDE (this one)
Fantastic Four
Thor
Spider Man
X-men
Metamorpho (and a few other comic books)
Thunder Agents (drawn by Wally Wood!)
The Realist
16
Cosmopolitan
Creepy and Eerie (Many old e.c. artists)

There's a number of magazines I seldom buy, but always read other peoples: *Life, Look, Scientific American*.

It's fun to listen to the radio with ears half shut--they were just playing "Shake Me, Wake Me", which stinks, and it sounded like a masochist litany.

Yes, the trickle-down theory. It's about the way something goes from specialized knowledge to general knowledge--the famous lowest common denominator who sits at the bottom of it all with his cosmic catchers mitt. Example: first references to the Beat thing I saw were in the *Nation & New Republic* in the summer (August) of 1957. I was in Southern California in June of 1958 when I heard a radio blurb which started, "There's been a lot of talk lately about the Beat Generation..." By summer 1959, there was an article about the Beat Generation in *This Week* magazine and the word "beatnik" was current. That word sure copped the public mind. It was a case of timing. Mind-copping usually is timing--the Sputnik shot was right in between Beat articles by *The Nation* and *Playboy*.

Now radio is playing "Wiggle-Wobble" by Les Cooper and The Soul Rockers. His record "Let's Do The Boston Monkey" is one of the best things I ever heard. By the way, the hard bop revolution will not crack until sometime between 1967 and 1970. The Stones, Otis Redding, Yardbirds, etc., are the second wave of shock troops, so to speak. The first wave--Little Richard, Fats Domino, Ray Charles, etc.--cracked 10 years ago. *<The hard bop revolution was a concept of Antonia's. Unfortunately, it never happened.>*

1958 was the focal point for all kinds of funny stuff. Folk music cracked, the Beat thing, the concept of "Soul". There was a recession, "sick" humor cracked. It had been "underground" since 1956, like the Beats. Many scenes that had been separate joined during 1958 to 1962. "Old timey" was another 1958 crack.

The current old-timey-hippy-folkmusic-rock-motorcycle-leather-jacket scene is quite a hybrid. It is encompassing other scenes and is being encompassed by still other scenes.

The '20s was the decade of flaming youth, the '30s was the decade of the worker, the '40s was the decade of the average man or slob, the '50s was the decade of the neurotic, the '60s is the decade of the in crowd. <The phrase "counterculture" wasn't around yet.>

Volume V, No. 5 • April 24, 1966

As human thought is becoming more conceptual, data becomes camp.

<Half-century + later, I have no idea what this means. It sounds like Antonia. I have no idea what she meant.>

The other day I was talking to Philly Dawg Subtrafuge, the lead singer of an up-andcoming rock group, The Brass Monkeys. He had a lot to say on the subject.

"Don't mean a thing if it ain't got that swing," he rattled off, adding, "Foom is a word you don't meet every day."

Your Reporter: "What's going on here?"

Philly Dawg: "Total WAR AGAINST THE DETROIT MACHINE! It's a sign of the times."

Your Reporter: "Seems the whole pop music field has taken up politics."

Philly Dawg: "I never was much of a one for dictators myself, but I think the whole country should be run by electricity."

Your Reporter: (laughing) "Well, that would eliminate the element of human error!"

Philly Dawg: "Plastic. Everything's going to be made out of plastic."

Your Reporter: "Lately I've been eating a lot of Knorr's beef noodle soup..." (At this juncture, Your Reporter fell headlong over an extension cord that was connected to Death on the Highway, the Brass Monkeys' lead guitarist.) "Excuse me. I didn't mean to unplug your instrument."

Death on the Highway: (blank horrible silence.)

Philly Dawg: "It's all right. He's just been on this diet of turtle cum and radishes. Says it makes him think of the guitar in a totally different context."

Your Reporter: "How about you, Philly Dawg? Do you take anything special to improve your singing?"

Philly Dawg: "Yee Har Har!"

Your Reporter: "Actually, I would like to know where you got the name Brass Monkeys."

Philly Dawg: "It's an old blues term." Your Reporter: "Could you be more explicit?"

Philly Dawg: (His pupils slowly dilating in time to his story.) "Down in the Okefenokee Swamps there are things unknown to civilized man. The swamps are as old as time; the ferns saw the passing of the dinosaurs, the marsh gasses rise, and the wind whispers, "Who's to know? Who's to know?'"

Your Reporter: "I see."

Philly Dawg: "It's deeply personal."

(At this juncture, Your Reporter turned back to Death on the Highway, who had not looked up from his guitar since the other juncture. It was difficult to break the spell of his concentration, but I finally captured his attention by disconnecting him again.)

Your Reporter: "Your-uh-style and appearance seem to attract a great many of the young lady fans. Do you feel this may detract from your reputation as a musician?"

Death on the Highway: (He replied, but Your Reporter hesitates to report such a phrase. Then he re-plugged the amplifier, picked up his guitar, and resumed his incomprehensible stream of sounds.)

Your Reporter: "Well, Philly Dawg, how much of your success do you feel you owe to the Little Guy--you know, the Man in the Street?"

Philly Dawg: "None. The trouble with the common man is, he's common."

Your Reporter: "What is it about the common man that makes him so...well...common?"

Philly Dawg: "The common man is absolutely structurally incapable of having a revelation."

Your Reporter: "And this is one of the things that you feel makes the Brass Monkeys special?"

Philly Dawg: "Yes, I have this feeling. We have lots of revelations, especially at breakfast and on tour."

Your Reporter: "Is there some final summation you'd like to give the public before we end this interview?"

Philly Dawg: "Stand back! I ain't finished with my crazy dance!"

Volume V, No. 7 • May 25, 1966

GOOD NEWS! CHARIOT'S COMING!

However, there's a man going round taking names. However, there's a name going round taking men, and it ain't likely to be put off much longer. Burroughs (William S. Burroughs) is RIGHT! Not totally, but what the hell. (April reported cruelest month--October, February, protest.) *Pearls Before Swine*, or *God Bless You, Mr. Rosewater*, by Kurt Vonnegut, Jr., is out. He wrote *Cat's Cradl*e, etc. In PAPERBACK--75¢

INCREDIBLE book by TOM WOLFE--*KANDY KOLORED TANGERINE FLAKE STREAMLINE BABY* out in paperback. I stumbled on two of his articles by most happy accident a year ago, and got boggled. One was about Las Vegas and was the first coherent piece on Las Vegas I ever saw. Next one I read by him was on stock car racing in the south-- like about the headset of North Carolina mountain people and how it comes out in the personality, driving style, etc., of stock car driv- er, and hundreds of other things! *Later made into a movi*e, The Last American Hero. So good to read, kind to ears, avuncular towards your LOBES. Highest ***** Rating.

Also, *The Maker Of Universes*, by Philip Jose Farmer. GAS par- allel universe megalomaniac book. LOVE books like that. I've been a Heinlen fan for years. Writes great ones like that. I like books that make me feel better, that get me off. I decided that's the only esthetic standard I'm going to use. Actually, it's the same ol' standard I've been using for years, but I never thought about it. DOES IT GET YOU OFF? Apply to books, pictures, noses, fireplugs, you know, the works.

"The WORKS?"
"THE WORKS!"
GLOMP!

"Watch it...There's a couple over there..."

Got the album by The Mamas & The Papas and played it dozens of times. They're GOOD! Flip side of "MONDAY, MONDAY" is just as good. Called "I've Got A Feelin'"--just as good. (I'm eating this great apple...) Sure like apples. Ideally hard, green, midwestern apples. Sigh! We used to bop up in the trees with salt shakers, and eat apples salted.

For Easter we got a FINE record by the IMPRESSIONS called "TOO SLOW" and found FLIP SIDE JUST FINE--now I like it better. Easter indeed! Others, current and crunchy:

"Shape of Things"--Yardbirds
"8 Miles High"--Byrds
"I'm a Roadrunner"--Jr. Walker & All Stars
"Wang Dang Doodle"--Koko Taylor
"Hold On, I'm Coming"--Sam & Dave
"No Man Is An Island"--Van Dykes
"GREETINGS (this is Uncle Sam)"--Monitors
"Searching For My Baby"--Bobby Moore

Also like Dylan "Rainy Day Woman", one I first heard while asleep and dreaming. That was fun.

Just got the Howlin' Wolf record with the rocking chair on it. He's fine. He learned to play from Charley Patton. Also got Yardbird-Sonny Boy Williamson record. It's good and very interesting to compare with their other two great records because this was recorded first.

The last two records--"I Want Someone" and "I Don't Have To Shop Around"--by the MAD LADS are two of the finest records I've ever heard. In both cases, the flip is great. Notice almost all great records have great flips? Example: "Going Home" on the back of Mickey & Sylvia's "Love Is Strange" and the last five Stones' records. Their latest, "Paint It Black" is so good. Their upcoming album (released now in England, I think) has a cut of them yelling and playing! SAME CHORD for 11 minutes and they cut it to five or seven. VERY VERY INTERESTING.

The MAD LADS--We saw them do a show with OTIS REDDING, who besides everything else is this big strong cat. MAD LADS dressed in YELLOW with BAGGY SLEEVES! So glad it's going back to that. One of my happiest memories was seeing the Little Richard show in 1957. His band wore PURPLE & ORANGE. YEAH! THE MANHATTANS also have had two hits in a row, and like the MAD LADS are not played on pop radio. Like I said, if Noah was a program director, he'd throw out the horses to make room for the warthogs.

Also there's a new record by the Hollies, who like The Who, are hardly played here. Do those program-directing people know what they're messing with? These as well as other questions...

If you haven't read *NOVA EXPRESS*, by Burroughs, read it. He's one of the best writers going.

Volume V, No. 9 • June 22, 1966

I'm doing this in May. Time is so fast now that, for instance, I could mention current good 45s that would be archaic by the time this is printed.

Here's two lists. How I love to make lists! Eventually maybe doing the whole column on lists. There's, for instance, the GIMME LIST which is a petition to the Cosmos, so to speak, and everybody has made activity lists. Ha-Ha.

Lists! To Port! Down to the sea in lists! Shopping lists! Christmas Card lists! DIDN'T YOU READ MCLUHAN YET WHO I HOLLERED ABOUT LAST SUMMER? READ HIM QUICK BEFORE IT'S TOO LATE--BUT NEVER MIND. TIME DOES NOT EXIST.

(EXTRA: As reported by James Joyce in '30s and McLuhan in 1962 and many others in between. Da whole planet--the whole planet? Even Sardinia! Even Steven! Yes? Yes?)

WHOLE SHEBANG REVERTING TO TRIBAL BASIS!

"Is that all?"

"Whut kinda basis is dat?"

"I don't know...he looks normal..."

TRIBAL BASIS DAMMIT! and that's why vast recent increase in:

1. Indian costume fashion influence
2. Tribal Style dancing!
3. FOLK MUSIC BOOM! CRASH!
4. Etc.!
5. Drums! Beat! Ho Ho Ho!
6. Connie Francis should be shot.

Brand new addition to famous CREEP LIST!

Bobby Kennedy (that jive punk) *<On list because of his anti-drug stance>*
Lord Byron *<Huh?>*
Harry Anslinger & Caligula
Virgil *<What!?>*
John Milton *<I had recently read Robert Graves' book, Wife to Mr. Milton, in which he was portrayed as a creep indeed, a quite nasty one.>*
Nancy Sinatra *<Take it back>*
Lou Christie *<Take it back>*
Marquis DeSade *<I'm sick of those fools who defend him.>*
J. D. Salinger (His fans worship a family who worships a suicide. The essence of the 1950s.)
Jackson Pollock (another suicide) *<I was very judgy about suicides.>*
The Shades of Knight *<Mediocre rock group. Harmless actually.>*

(Clouds gather, golden and silent. Cherubs flutter to earth shrieking "BALM! BALM!" and hurling viscous clots at passers-by.)

NICE LIST

Part one, been here awhile:

Cool Jerk--The Capitols
Sweet Talkin' Guy--Chiffons
Oh, How Happy!--Shades of Blue
Dirty Water--Standells

Part two, recent:

River Deep, Mountain High--Ike & Tina Turner
Little Girl--Syndicate Of Sound
Paperback Writer & Rain--Beatles
Elvira--don't know who did it
Take Time Out For Love--Isley Brothers
A Lover's Prayer--Otis Redding
You Better Run--Rascals

A few months ago, I touted a book called *Only Lovers Left Alive*. You've probably heard the Stones are going to do it as a movie. *<They were. Obviously fell through.>*

Two more, recent paperbacks:

The Sterile Cuckoo, by John Nichols. The writer is 24 and has written a very good, very funny, very accurate, boy-girl relationship study. Avon, 75¢.

I Am The Beautiful Stranger, by Roaslyn Drexler. Incredible gawp city schizophrenic dialogue by young teenage girl--or maybe not, there's a great deal of reality shifting. Am personally fond of reality shifts. Wheee...TERRY SOUTHERN says, "The best book I have read in a very long time." Dell, 60¢

Both these books are very good and fun as hell to read.

Summertime...Livin' Easy...

Summer Time, Summer Time, Sum Sum Summer Time...

In The Good Old Summertime...

Lazy Hazy Crazy Days of Summer...

Most Wonderful Summer of My Life...

WAIT 'TIL SEPTEMBER, YOU WON'T RECOGNIZE THE PLACE.

<This turned out to be true, mainly because by then we were both suffering from toxic psychosis.>

Volume V, No. 14 • August 31, 1966

Late night. Blind Justice Doolittle and Death on the Highway are wandering about the deserted wharfs of the city. A time of fog and blue neon haze.

The dampness in the air becomes more tangible--a huge squishing is heard in the distance, as of a million mops rising up out of the sea.

"IT'S THE GLOM!," says Blind Justice, who has a categorical mind.

The squishing is louder. Before it pulse waves of deep sea bottom ooze odor; the smell of things that were rotting when the world was young. Suddenly it rises up before them--132 feet high, grey-white in color, like an amoeba with teeth. It prepares to flop down on them and absorb them.

Death on the Highway whips out his ever present guitar and plays the 9 chord Infinity Loop Progression; momentarily trapping the Glom in a temporal moebius strip. As the Glom turns itself inside out, Justice says, "Let's get the hell out of here!"

But Death is engrossed in watching the results of his action. By now the Glom has gone most of the way through the loop and is turning itself right side out again. Blind Justice is thinking fast. "Hey," he asks, '"How much energy you got?"

Death almost grins and turns his guitar up a little louder.

"How long do you think you can keep playing that damn progression?"

"#*¢&%*#¢," says Death and commences to play at his usual unbearable pitch and speed.

Justice runs for a phone booth and zaps Brass Monkey headquarters. The others pour in from various strange night-points in the city. They are just in time to clean up the mess. The Glom has turned itself inside out so often and so fast that it is dead of exhaustion, and all that is left is a huge foul rotten four-foot layer of gooey-slime that covers six city blocks...

****

RETURN OF VEER CITY RIDER

I've been on a small strike because of the way Wilson's been hacking this column up. These things are constructed as units and taking pieces off defaces them. Especially after Wilson's nonsensical line about little publications being the only places where people could say "the truth" or something. Leave your bloody hands off this thing or I won't send any more. *<I was never paid anything for them, nor were other contributors, but we got a lot of good exposure.>*

In the meantime, I'm making a small neat pile of columns so they'll be there.

This summer has been licken' good records summer. One of the best yet. Many great records, but here are three that everyone should buy and play for days. If you happen to have them handy, play them over and over in a row while reading this, "cause I"m doing it while writing this...this...this...this? Duality freaking again. This and not this. That great team!

THE RECORDS ARE:

1. "5-D" and "Captain Soul", by the Byrds
2. "Sunny Summer Afternoon" and "I'm Not Like Everybody Else", by The Kinks

3. "Mr. Dyingly Sad" and "It Just Won't Be That Way", by The Critters

<Decades later I talked to McGuinn about "5-D". He said the melody was based on an old sea chantey and that its amazing instrumental outro was Van Dyke Parks.>

"5-D" (the fifth dimension) is about how to survive in space among other things. Great tune based on infinity type chord progression (of which there are an infinite number). Great words. The tune, words, rhythm of these three records all move towards the same end. This accounts for their power. "5-D" has been banned in Connectectigut? Conedgarput? Connurdigurd? Snodedergrass? That dumb state between here (New York) and there (Boston). Because it's supposed to be a "drug song."

"What kind a song is dat?"
"Dat's a song about Skruggs."
"No, dat's a Skruggs song, hee, hee."
"Rug songs? Bug songs?"
"Froog songs? Droog songs? Toad songs?"

The mad record banner rampages 'round, shrieking ban them all! Ban them all! They murk a malarky of our leisure fetishes! Dare gwine ter rot our minds like a mushmelon and toe jam!

The Critters record has a bass line that grunts like an alligator in the mud.

Continued next issue!

Volume V, No. 15 • September 14, 1966

Anybody who puts down The Troggs or The Shondells is a dope. Crispian St. Peters is the Wide Diaper. *<One-hit wonder who's hit, "The Pied Piper", I hated.>* Incidentally, I put down "Hanky Panky" until I listened to it closely--very fine lead guitar work.

I was gushing about "Mr. Dieingly Sad", "Sunny Afternoon" and "5-D"--I got hung on these records in June-July. On the current Billboard hot 100 "Sunny Afternoon" is 34 and "Mr. Diengly Sad" is 54. "5-D" is not on the chart but made the top 30 although it was not played in most of the country. We only heard it on WKBW in Buffalo which when we hear it--10 pm to 6 or 7 am--is the best pop station I have ever heard. Hooray for dial freaking engineers!

Gotta get my hands on a typewriter. "Sunny Afternoon" does a thing that has long been a big personal hit: to combine old and new sound in which the old sound was fairly accurate. Most people playing older forms of music play them too cute or too simple, mostly because they never really listened to older forms. Listen CLOSELY! Most people should be locked in a room and made to listen to the Harry Smith Anthology for 6 months.

Charley Patton
Charlie Poole
Make you quiver
Make you drool

In late 1961, when I was working at the Gaslight for a couple of months, I wore this old button that read, "You Can't Lose Me, Charlie." It was for, I think, Sweet Caporal Cigarettes. I was a Charlie Poole freak then but I had never heard of Charley Patton. *<Actually I had. He's on the Smith Anthology as the Masked Marvel, playing a song, "Mississippi Boll Weevil Blues", that I eventually covered with Hubby Jenkins.>*

All three of these records have great flips. The Kinks do "I'm Not Like Anybody Else", copying at least four other groups with uncanny accuracy.

****

Wow! Saturday night in Greenwich Village! Truly an adventure for the brave and/or foolhardy. We've been listening to and experimenting with electric-type music, so we braved the weekend crowds to find some. We were amply rewarded at the Nite Owl cafe, which is currently featuring two of the more interesting new groups. One bunch is called THE LITTLE FLOWERS, and their sound is sort of old-timey and country blues with electric instrumentation. They write a lot of their own stuff, too. Happy sounding stuff--makes you feel good.

<I had forgotten all about The Little Flowers. There's no sign of them on YouTube or Wikipedia. Another interesting sounding group eaten by Oblivion.>

The other group is LOTHAR AND THE HAND PEOPLE. They're kind of electronic and experimental without ever losing sight of what good music is, which is a fine trick. I guess they're based in rhythm & blues, though it's hard to say for sure (that's a compliment).

The whole business of filing music by category is pretty silly, anyway. Thank God everything good is just Music now, and all those damn labels have been outdated. It takes longer to categorize and trace back the new music ideas than it does to play or hear them, and it's a lot less fun. Next time somebody asks you, "What kind of music is that?," tell them it's TASMANIAN PLAID or something.

Volume V, No. 16 •September 28, 1966

THE FLESH EXPRESS
by Obscure Publishing Company

I

I said 'splain that to me, Kingfish
but he didn't explain
There's a sound going round
and it sounds like a train
It runs through the middle
of the radio dial
Out to space, in to earth
going faster all the while.
It rolls through the wires

and vibrates through the air
Inside out through itself
it keeps moving everywhere.
Was it put there by the Russians
just to mess up our minds
Did it happen by itself
Was it purposely designed
Some radio engineer freaking with his dials
Or an uptight mathematician with bleeding piles.
Is it good, is it bad, is it ours, is it theirs
Is it real, am I mad, was it God that put it there
What it is I don't know but I know that it is
And as long as it is I'll be part of it.
CHORUS:
I'm gonna ride ride ride ride
Ride ride ride ride
Ride ride ride the flesh express.

II

You seem to imagine that you want me to explain
But it might take forever for a thing to reach your brain.
You spend so much time thinking of what it might be
Analyzing, criticizing, making lists, telling me
And with all that stuff inside your head going round
I doubt if your ear ever got to hear the sound.
Go back to your room, that's the way to begin
Wear a gag and a blindfold and lock yourself in
Turn on your radio, turn on your brain
And don't move until you turn into that train

REPEAT CHORUS

<One of our shared hallucinations involved The TRAIN. We'd hear excited voices on the radio saying, "The train is coming." In our drug-crazed minds, the train was this great worldwide musical collective that was going to save the world, somehow. The train had a boss, who was, of course, called "the engi-

neer". We visualized him as our savior. Obviously, we were delusional.>

Volume V, No. 17 • October 12, 1966

Rain rain rain. That's all it's done for about 5 days now. We 're sitting in our slum, burning incense so there will be some smell besides WET DOG. We have no dog, but all slums smell of WET DOG when it gets damp.

A sign on the back of my notebook flashes before my eyes.

DON'T JUST STAND THERE--NOVA!

And I sit down to write this column.

I want to pass something exciting along. So I will tell you about the Raves.

The Raves are a bunch of electric musicians. Their number varies--right now, I think there's four of 'em. They're playing at the Cafe Wha in N.Y.C. now. The hard core of the group are Mike & Dave Rave (that's what they're called). Two brothers. Mike is lead singer, who doubles on drums, and Dave is lead guitarist. These two also balance each other, and the music. The music! They can really get you jumping up and down and yelling. They COMMUNICATE. And the teeny-boppers love them. Their scope is partly in their lack of pretension: they know they're making good music and they don't have to come on. What a refreshing thing to see and hear .

The Wet Dog smell is almost gone. Just the mention of people like the Raves helps to clear the air. Frankincense burned on charcoal helps, too. Also Van Van oil with John the Conqueror root. (We've been patronizing the Spanish botanicas in the neighborhood.)

Actually, we need all the good vibes we can get. We're in the difficult process of forming an electric-type group ourselves. Peter Stampfel is now an electric bass player (announcement). And the SWAMP LILIES are struggling toward formation & birth. We have the services of FREDDY, an ace rhythm guitarist, to help us along. *<Freddy was our speed supplier.>* And this week may bring in our drummer--and then we're OFF TO THE RACES!

Hey--listen to David Blue's album. It must be released by now. One of the most interesting songwriters on earth, I guess.
What'll I say to finish this half? Oh yes.
LISTEN TO THE YARDBIRDS.

****

UNPRECEDENTED UNPRECEDENTED MUSICAL DEVELOPMENTS continue to send shock wave after shock wave through the industry!

"Haven't those damn maniacs shut up yet? They've been playing for three days."

"Three days? I thought it was five."

"What the hell's happened to the radio?"
(WMCA just played the Marcels' "Blue Moon", 1961, and the Tokens' "Lion Sleeps Tonight", 1962. Dates, hahaha, dates...)

We're working on a bigger article on LOTHAR & THE HAND PEOPLE.

"Dates?"

"I want to know what the hell happened to Wednesday & Thursday."

"How should I know? All of a sudden this light flashed and a big jet flew over real low and two helicopters and Riley Puckett in a biplane."

"All the clocks are telling different times."
"And the smell--sort of a reek of--burnt metal."

"TWO WEEKS AGO I COULDN'T SPELL BLUE DINOSARE & NOW I ARE ONE"--Philly Dawg Subtrafuge

...finally this Puce Zeppelin on its way to a custom blimp festival in Wildwood, New Jersey. Then lightning & thunder...

Rain rain rain. That's all it's done for about five days now.

Volume V, No. 18 (& Antonia) • October 26, 1966

There's a man going 'round making trains; or, Rider, see what you done done:

Suddenly, from nowhere, New York City is covered with squadrons of caterpillars. Where did they come from? No one knows. But I've been told that they'll turn into moths. Better pray for another big rain.

For those who are interested, Van Van Oil combined with John the Conquerer root can be obtained from The House of Candles, 99 Stanton Street, N.Y.C. Frankincense, too.

Assorted objects time: just purchased a day-glo stick-on sign for our mirror that says DREAM BIG. That seemed to be a good thing for a mirror. Also decorating our instruments with buttons and diffraction gratings. Part of getting set for the work season (cold weather). And today's cleaning turned up an official U. S. Army tuning fork. What hath God wrought?

Speaking of the official U.S. Army and stuff like that, there's a dumb fad going around here of people carrying pistols and stuff. Oddly enough, these are the same people who are always getting in trouble.

Back to Music. AH! (Sigh of relief). Yes, we said we would tell more about Lothar and the Hand People. Yes, there is such a group, check with the Nite Owl Cafe here if you don't believe me. Lothar is a theramin. He (she? it?) is played by John, who also sings lead. Also very much in evidence are Kim King on lead guitar, Paul on rhythm guitar, Rusty Ford on bass and Tom Flye on drums. I don't believe those names either, but they're all real. They came together from all parts of the country to form LOTHAR AND THE HAND PEOPLE on January 1, 1966. They make MUSIC. What else can I say? Agitate to get these people into the Cambridge area and see for yourself.

Jesse Colin Young and the Youngbloods have just finished cutting their record for RCA Victor. A tremendous amount of work and talent have gone into this, and it should be something special. More on this later.

Oh well, time to put some more incense on the fire. This is a hell of a way to run a railroad.

****

SWAMP LILIES GO FOURWARD (not to mention slideways): Now we are tentatively four. Eddie the drummer appeared on the Swamp Lily doorstep last night. He will hopefully be working out with us in about 2 weeks--when we hope to have a place where we can rehearse with drums. Then, we'll get to hear what we all sound like together. Is the world ready for this? Bigger question--are we? Meanwhile, Freddy and us are continuing our super-secret closed rehearsals. Well, it makes us feel important.

Boy, did I make a lot of funny discoveries this summer. To teach myself bass, I was playing the bottom four strings of a guitar since they are the same four notes as an electric bass only an octave higher. I would play with the radio or records. This is perhaps the easiest way to learn. Anyway, I was playing with a record of country blues and nothing worked until I tuned the guitar one full tone lower so the bottom was D instead of E. And once I did that, I did the same damn lick for the last five cuts of the album. Then I turned on the radio and it played "Paperback Writer" and it fit perfectly. Then the radio played "I Saw Her Again" and the same lick worked again. Been trying to draw a conclusion ever since. But I've decided to tune my bass one full tone lower than standard. Next issue I'll tell about the Grand Monochord of the Universe!

TIME IS ON THE SLIDE!

Volume V, No. 19 (& Antonia) • November 9, 1966

MOTION TIME! Fight Terminal Stasis! Move NOW! Jump up and down and make music all night. FEEDBACK LIVES! Treat it kindly--it'll do the same for you sometime.

Recording contracts fallin' down like rain. The Raves are recording for Laurie Records today, and we hear that Capitol has signed Lothar and the Hand People. WAHOO! Maybe that will end the wave of galloping crud that is now engulfing the airwaves. If I hear one more bloody Motown record that sounds like every other Motown record...

Thank God for the few moving records around: Joe Cuba's "Bang Bang," "Good Vibrations," "Ain't Nobody Home", "Winchester Cathedral."

SWAMP LILIES NOVA: Radical shakedown in the lineup now has Peter on bass, Bill Barth on guitar, Nancy Jeffries on vocals, and our manager on tranquilizers.

We've been getting up in the morning lately, just like daypeople. What a multi-level bringdown. It's cold in the morning, and everybody is surly and short-tempered. The only way to survive is by putting on the record player LOUD and eating beef noodle soup. Wonder what people did to wake up before record players happened? Faked it, I guess. Us, too. It's down with the beef noodle soup and then blindstagger out into the crashing daylight, singing, "How is it that I could come out to here and be still floating?" A good question indeed.

Soon we find ourselves in the subway where we read the daily augury. The subway's a good place for that. Lots of entrails to read and all those cryptic messages on the walls. Feedback City. It's a wonder anybody goes above ground. You could stay there forever, just watching the tides. And the minute you go down there, you're rid of that damned nuisance: Time. This factor alone is worth the price of admission. Been looking for a simple way to get rid of Time for years, and here the New York Transit Authority has done it without half trying. Ah, technology.

Goin' to Slurp City
Where there's boxes and dials
And you can hear a pin drop
For miles and miles
Next week: Fuzz Tone comes to the Swamp!

****

Dave Rave of the Raves is easily one of the best and most interesting guitarists in New York City. Kim King is another one of these. Kim is the lead guitarist for Lothar and the Hand People. Dave, I believe, started playing rock guitar but watched the different things people used in the Village: folk-type chord patterns, finger picking and all the incredible hybrids. Kim started out in folk music--he appeared at the Newport Folk Festival. Their styles, like the styles of all "Ace" guitar players, are way different. Both Dave and Kim are also fun as hell to watch while they play.

Great Shakes, that unbelievable beverage with the song that sounds like, you know:

Every house can be a soda fountain now
With Ape Shake, new Ape Shake

Anyhow I just had one for the first time and it's great.

The Youngbloods have cut their single record; "Grizzly Bear" on one side, "Tears" on the other. Watch for this one.

I just sat down to write this a half hour ago and since then I had my first Great Shake(s?), and ESP Records called and said they bought this tape me and Weber and the Fugs cut with Harry Smith in March 1965. It has five things with me and Weber alone as well as those early Fug classics, like "Coca Cola Douche", "We're the Fugs" (GREAT song), and (F***ing A Man) "C.I.A. Man", as well as two of my early works, "Romping Through the Swamp" and "New Amphetamine Shriek". Wow, is that going to be a record.

Man of the Year--1965
MICK JAGGER

Man of the Year--1966
JEFF BECK

(Next issue: What's a Jeff Beck?)

Volume V, No. 20 (& Antonia) • November 23, 1966

I just watched the sunrise. Wow. All this stuff about watching the sun come up being edifying and enlightening is cow flop. In winter, anyway. It's all grey, like clam soup or something. And the music they play on the radio in the early morning is enough to make you hide under the bed. Only WKBW in Buffalo remains in motion, and our reception starts fading out around this time.

At last, a good book out in paperback: *Marie Beginning*, by Alfred Grossman. Sort of a black comedy morality play. A pleasant change from all those suburban neurosis and Nazi concentration camp novels.

TULI KUPFERBERG IS A POET! And ESP Records is releasing his "Morning, Morning" as a single record. Smart move. Record #4508.

The Youngbloods: Jesse Colin Young on bass, Jerry Corbitt on guitar, Joe Bauer on drums, and the incomparable Banana on piano and occasional guitar. Vocals by Jesse and Jerry. We mentioned their record, but stupidly forgot to rave about their stage act. Will do so now. They're tight. They're frequently found at the Cafe a Go Go here in New York .

Metaphysical Bullshit Department: Yesterday I tried something called Congo Bath. Put it in the bath water, which turned slimy pink. The whole mess smelled disgusting, but I thought, oh well, and got in. The water promptly turned a nice brownish pink color and smelled just fine. When I got out I felt GREAT and full of energy, like my batteries were recharged. It's the next morning now, and I still feel good, but the bathtub stinks.

Sure have been a lot of "flying saucers" sighted lately, haven't there? I was talking to a news photographer this morning who said that he had just taken pictures of some, and the Air Force had verified the sightings; he said he didn't know what they were, but a big news story would be breaking soon.

Carol Hunter has written a "Triumphal March For Those Who Walk in 5/4 Time". She's one of those rare beings who radiates from the inside.

Wow! Chamomile tea! Is that how you spell it? My grandmother used to make it, and I tried some today. It's great tasting stuff and good for cold weather. You can get it at the drugstore.

"Gee, we were going to write a column about Jeff Beck."

"And I was supposed to write one about the Grand Monochord of the Universe." It'll have to be a separate column. It'll take at least a column to talk about Jeff Beck."

"I couldn't think of a whole column of things to say about Jeff Beck."

"I sure could."

"I wouldn't mind reading a whole column on Jeff Beck but I don't think most people would want to do that."

"Everyone wants to read a whole column on Jeff Beck. He's the most copied guitar player in the world. Everyone is talking about him."

"Well, I couldn't write more than a few hundred words about Jeff Beck without getting pornographic."

"Great! Do it!"

"No, we couldn't consider it."
"I've already considered it. Let's do it!"

"No, the Yardbirds' lawyer could sue us for libel or something..."

Short pause.

"But then we could get to meet Jeff Beck."

TYGER LIL'S INCENSE WORKS. Three yummy flavors. Electric Banana, Hoochy Koochy and Jeff Beck.

Volume V, No. 21 (& Antonia) • December 7, 1966

RED ALERT! Good records being buried under the crudwave on the radio. Seek them out! For instance, the Critters have quietly slipped in a new entry called "Bad Misunderstanding", which is a perfect little gem of a record and you hardly hear it anywhere. "Talk Talk", by the Music Machine, is yet to be heard in our area. Then there's the new Yardbirds "Happenings 10 Years Time Ago", the record that answers the burning question--is Jeff Beck really the Eggplant that ate Chicago? As a substitute for all this jelly, we are offered Ronnie Dove and Nancy Sinatra and the Outsiders. FAUGH.

Also, I like Question Mark and the Mysterians and Neil Diamond and "Bend It". Do they play "Bend It" on the air in Boston? They don't in N.Y.C., but they do in Buffalo. Good smut-rock is hard to find. Good smut of any kind is hard to find. There are all these books with sex, I mean, but nobody has much fun at it and everybody's neurotic and it's hard to get your prurient interest aroused, even. If sex was that big of a hassle, I don't think many people would bother, unless they were masochists. Peter Willow is a good smut writer. He writes for a company called Original First Niter Books (honest!).

Two good books--HOORAY--after all this time with nothing to read! *Night of Light*, by Philip Jose Farmer (sort of about religion), and *The Night Clerk*, by Stephen Schneck (sort of about love).

There are a number of groups working out of California who haven't cracked here yet. Two of the prime ones are the Buffalo Springfield and the Seeds. We have had the Springfield's "Nowadays Clancy Can't Even Sing" on order at our record store for months. I just bought the Seeds' first album *A Web Of Sound* on the Crescendo label. It's very hard rock, something like the first Them album, but even better. *No, it wasn't.* Skillful use of strange sounds and organ. This is where hard rock groups mess up the most. You need taste to use feedback or organ effectively. The Seeds have taste. Easily one of the best groups in the country.

A number of the most important books ever written have recently appeared in paperback or have been re-issued in new and cheaper editions:

The White Goddess--Robert Graves
Naked Lunch--William Burroughs
Understanding Media--Marshall McLuhan

New Love album, *Da Capo*, due for release soon. Some good new single records:

Little Black Egg--The Night Crawlers
<Can be found on the first Lenny Kaye/Elektra/Nuggets collection.>
Long Hair--Tony & Sigrid
Fifi the Flea--Sidekicks

I Need Someone--Question Mark and the Mysterians

Incidentally, the two songs I wrote won't be on the new Fugs album because the ESP Record boss insisted on half the publishing rights. Such a piggy record man. Speaking of piggy record men, Koppelman & Rubin owe me several hundred dollars for "Blues in the Battle", my version of which is on the first Spoonful album. They are currently being sued because that's the only way to deal with their ilk.

<I eventually got $3000 from John Sebastian. Still my all-time music $ score. And those were 1968 dollars. I bought a Vega White Lady banjo for $150. Be around $4000 nowadays.>

Where are all the honest record makers? 97% of all record company executives pass their time doing the toe jam circle suck. "Nothing like thinking on your feet," one was heard to remark as he wiped his mouth with a Kleenex.

Volume V, No. 22 (& Antonia) • December 21, 1966

Summer is gone. Winter officially broke its back as a Thanksgiving treat. Son of murky lurkey turkey. Revenge of Nameless Horror. But we had our day this summer, and a fine one it was, too. Long and warm and full of--you know--everything. We've been doing experiments in musical alchemy in deepest earnest, pressing the frontier of knowledge and experience on, sailing on, through thick and thin, pennants bravely fluttering, then tautly vibrating as the wind from outer space approached the sound barrier. "Excelsior!," we chanted.

The black riders of Mordor plagued us, hiding in our heads and accusing us of witchcraft and seduction of the innocent. The innocents in question plagued us with sonic booby traps that, when sprung, emitted gargantuan farting noises. "How is it that I can come out to here and still be floating?," we kept asking the crowded empty rooms while the Flying Circus and Floating Opera called from outside.

The flashing crashing songs chased each other zodiacally across the summer sky, a pinwheel of stars...a galaxy holds its breath and prays for nova. *<We were taking fucktons of speed.>*

And it is after midnight, the first of December, and Nashville, Cincinnati and Buffalo are playing king of the mountain on the end of my radio dial. *<They were all 50,000 watt stations located about the same spot on the AM dial. Occasionally, if the weather was right, a Waterloo, Iowa station would join the fun.>*

WOR-FM, New York's FM pop station plays the country top 40, R&B top 40, and Latin top 40 as a regular Saturday feature. Roman candle salute and Banzai bouquet, good people.

Hey, wanna try something WEIRD? Got an electric guitar, kid? OK, plug it in. Fine, leave it plugged in but don't play it. Let music happen around it, radio, records, you, etc. Don't play the left-on guitar. Just let it be for three or four days, plugged in and on all the while. I'd tell you what happens next but you wouldn't believe me. *<Only works if you've been taking a lot of speed.>*

COMPLAINT DEPT: Take time, now. (Yes, but where?) It's funny stuff. First of all, it doesn't exist. Eternity exists. Time is something invented by the human mind. It's the old power play game. Do you have time right now, or does time have you? When I have time by the tail, for example, guitar and writing and such are easy. When time has me, I might as well knock off and read comics for a while, because I know I caught myself in my own trap again. People invented time to help them deal with eternity and now find themselves having to deal with time, too. What??!?? Down with this nonsense. JOIN THE MARCH ON TIME! In the next issue, we shall take up space.

While we're stomping things, let's get paranoia. There it is, under the bed. In the air, in your hair, everywhere. We have composed an appropriately convoluted anthem, sort of Gregorian-ragtime, for the occasion.

****BYZANTINE ROCK****

1.

Do I hear the voice of my Byzantine queen
Who calls from a country that never quite was
Across an abyss with my fears in between
And is she in my mind or am I in hers?
The chasm between us is deeper than sin
Its walls are a mountain thats turned inside out
By something that wants me to stay where I've been
And spends its time plotting against me, no doubt
Chorus:
Scheming Loretta and Plotting Frank
<The villains in the mid-20th Century radio soap opera, Mary Noble, Backstage Wife.>
And all of those others you never quite see
They're tapping the phone and they're watching the house
And I got a feeling they're out to get me.
Meanwhile back in Byzantium
The moon is always full and red
And someone that I almost know
Watches the inside of my head.

2.

My Queen is as dark as the midnight sky
I've not seen her face but I know she is fair
She whispers a secret that may be a lie
Or may be the truth if in truth she is there.
For women are born knowing how to deceive
And men are a greedy and treacherous lot
And I am the only one I can believe
Unless I should find myself part of the plot.

Repeat Chorus

1967

Volume V, No. 23 (& Antonia) • January 4, 1967

Picked up the new first album by the BUFFALO SPRINGFIELD. It's very good indeed, all original stuff. They sound like they've heard the Rounders, but I don't know. Five in number; three of them play guitar. Takes taste to run simultaneous guitars and super-taste to run more than two. Tasty Buffalo Springfield.

Finally copped the CRITTERS' first album a few weeks ago. Brilliant shining record. Ace construction and some of the best uses of vocal harmonies since the Ink Spots. Mostly original stuff, mainly by the rhythm guitarist, who is 19 and one of the best songwriters going. Such a listenable impressive record.

There's been talk about which blues band will crack on a pop level first. A local contender is WOODY'S TRUCK STOP, spawned in Philadelphia and recently migrated to Cambridge. They are still crystallizing into their final form (all groups have to put in a few laps in the crucible before the pieces are firmly in place). The Truck Stop has a fine hard blues sound and a sense of pretty. These two factors are seldom co-existent. Their basis is in blues, but I have no idea where they'll end up. They're not the kind of group that's going to stay in one place very long.

Attention Wally Wood freaks and Art Patrons! Wally Wood, one of the legendary E. C. Comics artists, and, in my opinion, one of the finest living artists on the planet, has put out his own magazine, WITZEND. It's great, incredible, beautiful and an absolute necessity. Gobble it, grope it. Send one dollar bill--please do not send checks, he requests; they're an awful hassle--per issue to:

Wallace Wood
Box 882
Ansonia Station
New York, N.Y.   10023

Al Williamson! Frank Frazetta! Reed Crandall! Yes, Virginia, there is a renaissance!

Books are coming back. Once again there are some good things around in paperback. First of all, anything written by Colette. What an alive woman! Then there's *Midnight Cowboy*, by Herlihy. A sad and beautiful book, and, reprinted, *The Sirens of Titan*, by Kurt Vonnegut, Jr. Lots of fun is this one. The Church of God the Utterly Indifferent??!??

Fuzz Tone is a whole other dimension. So is electric fiddle. Plans to combine the two are now under way in our household.

Calling all bears and other honey lovers. Try Rosemary Honey--obtainable in Cambridge fancy food stores. A superhigh.

Hang On Sloopy Dept.: This has been a bad year for most people, but the I-Ching and the Tarot both say...a change is coming with the winter solstice, which begins December 22. A move forward is predicted. Well, it's about time, I say.

Wahoo records of the week:

Going Nowhere--Los Bravos
I'm a Boy--The Who
Papa Was Too--Joe Tex
Pretty Ballerina--The Left Bank
Little White Lies--The Motley Blues Band

Tossup for the dullest record of the week is a tie between "Snoopy Vs. The Red Baron" and "Sugartown".

The Monkees are cute as a bug's ear and all that, but they don't play on their records. A group called the Magic Circle does the playing. *<On just their first album. All Them, after that.>*

For beautiful fever dreams, read J. G. Ballard.

NIGHT OWL STRIKES AGAIN! Joe Maraa, who runs the Night Owl Cafe in Greenwich Village, has a gold ear. He keeps turning up these good musical groups. The latest pack of winners working there is called the FLYING MACHINE, and they are, and they do. Everyone in the group is just fine. Two of them write their own songs ("Rainy Day Man" and the hilarious "I'm a Steamroller"). They also do one of the hardest versions of "Rock Me, Baby" I ever heard. The best song of the night, though, was Hoagy Carmichael's "Baltimore Oriole". The Flying Machine does blues, ragtime, ballads and modern jazz with equal facility, and that's saying a lot. And a good drummer for a change. There are very few good drummers around recently.

<The Flying Machine was James Taylor's first group, as in, "Sweet dreams and Flying Machines in pieces on the ground." This is the first instance I am aware of of a rock group covering a song from the Great American Songbook: "Baltimore Oriole". Unless you want to count the Beatles doing "'Til There Was You". Of course, many duo-wop groups covered GAS songs in the '50s: "Smoke gets in Your Eyes", "My Prayer", "When My Dreamboat Comes Home", etc.>

Movies are back. Or maybe we've just been away. But anyway, we caught a flick called Blow Up. Hooray! People who make movies are beginning to explore the whole question of responsibility and they're doing it with good direction, acting, and photography. May the Great Cosmic Duck shed his blessings liberally on everyone connected with *Blow Up*.

Incidentally, the Yardbirds are featured in Blow Up. What a weird looking bunch of people. You'll gasp as Jeff Beck destroys a guitar that won't feed back. Sic Semper Tyrannis!

One of the most useful music books I've ever seen is *Silence* by John Cage, published in paperback by MIT. It's slow going, but worth it. Full of useful odd information, like, when you're in a totally sound-proof room you'll hear two sounds, one high and one low. The high sound is your nervous system functioning and the low one is your bloodstream. Cage uses the word "silence" to mean all the random sounds that happen. Lothar and The Hand People call it "fnif fnaf". Speaking of the Hand People, there's a good continued series on them in *Hit Parader* magazine. *<Years later I found that John Cage was perhaps the first person in New York City to move into an industrial loft.>*

Strange Experience Dept: We've been without electricity for about a week now. The wiring in our slum is all rotted out, and mice run around in the wiring and get electrocuted. This has led to many new and thrilling experiences, such as playing non-electrified electric guitar and writing BROADSIDE columns by candlelight. Reading is a hassle, though, and so is tape recording. We have a borrowed Concord tape recorder. It weighs about 300 pounds. Don't ever buy a Concord. Buy a Burns guitar instead. I got a Burns and I want to see if it's true about all Burnses or just mine.

Super-Wahoo Record: "Baby Doll", by the Howard Street Station.

By now you've all got the Donovan *Sunshine Superman* album, right? Right.

CONTEST! CONTEST! Big fat super easy. Just write us a letter answering the question "who's driving this train, and why?" Best answer wins a box of genuine certified Amp Sweepings which when dumped over your instrument, will provide lots of high quality fnif fnaf. Send your letters to Peter Stampfel and Antonia, Apt. 1B, 309 East Houston Street, New York, N. Y. 10002.

****FEEDBACK LIVES*****

Volume V, No. 25 (& Antonia) • February 1, 1967

It was a slow day at Brass Monkey headquarters. Everybody was sick of winter, so Philly Dawg Subtrafuge had set the climate adjuster on "mid-summer", and now everyone was just sitting around and sweating. The only sound was the incessant yowl produced by Death on the Highway, his ever-present guitar, and his Feedback Laminator.

Suddenly, the trouble alarm sounded. Blind Justice Doolittle, most practical of the Brass Monkeys, pushed the Decode Button--there was a dry insect like rustling. Blind Justice fed this information into the electric Reason.

"It is the Chemical Nun," said the Electric Reason.

"How do we know it ain't you," asked Philly Dawg, who was feeling strange from all the feedback.
"Fod," said the Electric Reason, which had been programmed to give a silly answer to a silly question.

Death on the Highway looked up quizzically from his guitar.

"The Chemical Nun," said Blind Justice. "She wanders through the land, convincing young people that their bodies are evil. If that ain't enough, she gets 'em high on stuff that makes them believe it."

"To the rescue!," yelled Philly Dawg. The three of them headed for Northeast University, where the Chemical Nun was conducting a class in experimental psych. They could hear the chitinous rustling of her black robes as they approached the classroom.

Death on the Highway settled himself comfortably outside the classroom and began to play a seductive Dionysian theme on his guitar. Soon there was an annoyed flurry from the room and, preceded by a stale stench of unused pussy, the Chemical Nun herself emerged.

"Get her!," Philly Dawg hollered, and Blind Justice plunged home a hypodermic full of powerful female hormones...

Death and Blind Justice walked down the hall together, leaving the ex-Chemical Nun and Philly Dawg to bat their eyes at each other.

****

Patty LaBelle and the Bluebelles are back! At this writing, they're at the Apollo theatre in Harlem, but they usually play the whole East Coast at one swoop. As we've mentioned, they are the best chick singing group in the business. These girls were putting out psychedelic music before the hippies knew how to spell it. Imagine the Apollo theatre, sort of a rhythm and blues music hall uptown in N. Y. C.; the lights go down and here are these four distinctively beautiful chicks, each with a voice that would make a great lead singer, each dresses in a slightly out-of-date prom gown type of thing. They start singing and moving to their own music, and you don't need a light show.

They are a light show.

It's Bonanza Week here--the Youngbloods are at the Arthur and the Buffalo Springfield are at Ondine's. At least our fancy discotheques are hiring interesting people to play in them. I'm glad to see credit (and work) going to people who deserve it. Also the Youngbloods and Springfield have been enjoying each other's music since they met in California.

LOTHAR AND THE HAND PEOPLE ARE COMING! Yes, they exist. Right at the moment, Lothar-the-theremin and his five cohorts are going into the recording studio for three weeks, but by the time this hits print that formidable songwriting and musicproducing team will be headed for the Boston–Cambridge area. I told you it was good news week. They've been into numerous feedback experiments recently, too. Be on the lookout for Lothar and the Hand People!

Next Week--Country Joe and the Fish.

Volume VI, No. 1 (& Antonia) • March 1, 1967

FAKE SUMMER NOW! There's a great product out to do it with. The Carolina Soap and Candle Makers have something called "Carolina Wilde Strawberry Sachet". It comes in a spray can and you squirt it around the room and this sort of light strawberry rain comes down. Or spray in your bed and sleep in a strawberry patch. Yum. These people also make lemon shampoo, which makes the whole business of hair washing fun. All these things come in other smells, too, like bayberry and magnolia, but the fruits seemed most interesting. Maybe because we're waiting so hard for summer.

Then there's summertime eating Wisconsin cheddar cheese and tomatoes. Wow. And lots of Kool-Aid, which is a little hard to find at this time of year but worth the effort in sheer atmosphere. And wear lots of orange clothes, or yellow. It helps get that warm feeling. We'll make it through winter yet, by hook or by crook!

New albums out by the Stones, Beach Boys, Mamas & Papas, & Donovan. Heard the Stones and Donovan.

More Renaissance. The people that put out Captain Marvel comics have a comic book called Fatman, The Human Flying Saucer. The best and most influential comic book man is Will Eisner. He wrote and drew SPIRIT comics in the 1940s and is the main influence for the E. C. classics of the early '50s. Now he's doing it again for 25¢. Absolutely some of the finest artwork Western man has produced.

We got a treble booster and now we can boost trebles. What a good sound. Very crystalline.

I might buy a home-made fuzz tone. These produce a "dirtier" sound than commercial fuzz tones, which are lots of fun, too. Fuzz tones & treble boosters can be teamed up to produce sustained unbearable notes.

The Spencer Davis Group at last! How about the Who? And the Move? And the Cream? And Pink Floyd?

Lothar and The Hand People will have a record out by March 1. One side, "L-o-v-e", features theremin. *<The B side, "Let The Boy Pretend", was written by Hand Person Paul Conly and Antonia.>*

Mysterious Al Wilson, ex-BROADSIDE reviewer, is a member of a California blues band called the Canned Heat Blues Band.

Bill Barth & Nancy Jeffries have arrived in New York and the Swamp Lilies are back in rehearsal. Hooray! First tapes should be made this week. We're doing a lot of original material.

For them who are interested in the occult, here's a list of CANDLE COLOR MEANINGS, mainly courtesy of the House of Candles:

WHITE--good, purity
GRAY--uncrossing, victory over evil
BLACK--evil
RED--health, strength, love, physical matters
GOLD--attraction, success, magnetism money, crops, finance
BROWN--earth, reality matters
BLUE--the spirit world
ORANGE--concentration or dreams
PINK--happiness
YELLOW--spiritual enlightenment or revelation
PURPLE--power (very strong color)

We've been burning candles for assorted purposes since the summer, with good results. You put oil on a candle; what kind of oil will determine the results. Always oil candles from center to top and from center down to bottom. This is called "observing the laws of polarity". I don't know what happens if you don't. We've been doing it and just got new Ampeg amplifiers as a result.

<The main "purpose" we burned candles was to score speed, invoking magic. Sometimes the candle would simply let us know nothing was happening, like the time we checked it out and found that not only had it gone out, but there were two dead flies embedded in the hardened wax.>

FEEDBACK LIVES!

Volume VI, No. 3 (& Antonia) • March 29, 1967

A while back, we mentioned an amazing guitar player named Jimmy James, who was playing with a group called the Blue Flame at the

Cafe Wha. He never became too well known here, but now, under the name of Jimi Hendrix, he's quite well known in England. His flashy guitar-playing style is really knocking them out over there, and he's had a record in the top 10. Another well-deserved success. Onward and upward.

Wahoo albums: *Surrealistic Pillow* by the Jefferson Airplane; beautiful vocals on this one and taste, taste, taste. Yum. Personal favorite cut: "Comin' Back To Me". Then there's the Spencer Davis group album, *Gimme Some Lovin.* Anybody who likes hardrock sounds should invest in this album. One of the few good uses of organ I've heard.

The Swamp Lilies have acquired a rhythm guitarist, by the name of Alan Warshak. Also, we now have half of a demonstration tape, with more to follow soon.

Nice new Hollies Record. *On A Carousel.* It makes up for that summertime horror, "Stop Stop Stop", the second spookiest record after "Cherish". <*Think about: "I want to mold you into someone I can cherish".*> Also, Donovan has a new album out.

New Songs! We're writing all kinds of new songs. Wahoo for new material. Keeps you from getting bored. New titles: "Big Slop Buckets" and "For the Knight of Swords".

New Group! A really good jazz-based group: the Free Spirits. Saw them at the Balloon Farm, a big cold psychedelic-light-show-type place here in New York. They consist of Larry Coryell on guitar, Chip Baker on rhythm guitar and 12-string, Jim Pepper on tenor sax and flute, Chris Hills on bass and Bob Moses on drums. One of their sounds is two voices using modal 5th harmonies, another is the use of parallel sax and guitar lines.

Book plug: *Zap Gun*, by Philip K. Dick. Science fiction, out in paperback. About the use of hallucinogens for designing (weapons, fashions!) among other things.

Hey, we've been reading the Denver column, and we like it.

Lothar & the Hand People are on a songwriting kick, too. Should hit Boston with a lot of new material. They really tore up Philadelphia last weekend, and are anticipating Boston and the legendary Boston girls.

Yes, Dino Valenti. He was the most widely copied guitar player who ever played in the Village, besides Dylan. None of his imitators got the same excitement into their music, though. He's been playing in San Francisco recently. Haven't heard his recent work.

The Mothers are really good musicians. Nobody seems to have mentioned that in all the stuff I've seen written about them. Frank Zappa is an incredible guitar player and runs the Mothers like a captain runs a ship. It's a clean machine. They cover more ground than any other group, and can play accurately in more styles. They're one of the few groups who really knows how the old rock sound worked.

Style note for talented girls--make your old man some mod-style trousers, or Tom Jones shirts, out of upholstery fabrics. The patterns are great, and they'll last forever. Note--girl's pants are a lot easier to make than men's.

Volume VI, No. 5 (& Antonia) • April 26, 1967

Wow! We got an album by the Cream. It's called *Fresh Cream* and it includes their single "I Feel Free", one of the best records to come out this year. Other good cuts include "Rollin' and Tumblin'" and "Dreaming", but everything on the album is worth listening to. It's on the Atco label.

The Who are coming out with a new album this week, too. They're crazier than ever, with things on the album like "Boris the Spider" and "Cobwebs and Strange". Amazing music. The Who keep getting better all the time and they were good to begin with.

Wahoo records of the week:

"Happy Jack"--The Who
"On a Carousel"--The Hollies
"I Feel Free"--The Cream (This deserves to be mentioned twice)
I Got Rhythm"--The Happenings
"Rose-Colored Glasses"--Lothar and the Hand People
"Mirage"--Tommy James & The Shondells
"Hey Joe"--Jimi Hendrix Experience

New book out by Marshall McLuhan and Quentin Fiore, *The Medium is the Message*. A very graphic, pictorial book which illustrates its theory by its presentation. Besides summing up a lot of things about modern communication, McLuhan is fun.

It's Easter Time again, and Murray the K, a local disc jockey, is back with another show. This time he's had the good sense to bring The Who and The Cream over from England. It's about time someone did. He also broke the Ike and Tina Turner record "River Deep, Mountain High" on New York radio. This record was issued a year ago, made a hit in England over the summer, but never got airplay here. A terrific record.

Ugh. Petula Clark.

The 1967 Phlegm Leer award goes to gross oaf Mitch Ryder. Runners-up are Eric Burdon and Tom Jones. It was a close race, folks, but after "Sock It To Me, Baby", Mitch walks away with it. Tom Jones had it last year.

We also heard a number of cuts from the Doors album. The Doors are the most over-rated group since the Blues Project.

Kurt Vonnegut's (*Cat's Cradle*) first novel, *Player Piano*, is out in paperback.

Good new food--Contadina sliced baby tomatoes. Real good stuff.

Also Daisy's snack cereal.

We have a winner in the "Who's Driving This Train, and Why?" contest. Her name is Eliza, and her answer is nearly as cryptic as the question, but makes sense in this context. A can of amp sweepings will be on its way to her in about two weeks. We're currently engaged in a hunt for the proper can. We've got the amp sweepings.

People who play spooky things on the radio should be bricked off the air. A few nights ago, a local FM station broadcasted a bad LSD trip at 2 a.m., complete with musical sound effects. It woke us up with nightmares. I ask you, is that fair?

We leave the radio on all night. This is an excellent way to absorb a knowledge of music. Try it. You'll find yourself with more subconscious musical knowledge than you know what to do with. *<Antonia always slept with the radio on because it alleviated her chronic night horrors. I quickly got used to it when I moved in with her Christmas 1962.>*

Volume VI, No. 9 (& Antonia) • June 22, 1967

Album time! Looks like everyone has come up with a new album this month. As expected, the Who album is out, and is one of the finest songs around, There's a long cut at the end called "A Quick One While He's Away", that blends many forms of music into a sort of miniature operetta, There isn't a dull cut on the album, and the Who are better than ever. That's saying a lot.

We also got to hear part of the new Country Joe & The Fish album. What fine guitar playing on this one. A new version of "Section 43", a long instrumental, is included. Another A-1 job is "The Death Sound", a beautiful blues piece. I'm anxious to hear the rest. I heard about half.

"Hey Joe", by Jimi Hendrix has finally been released as a single record.

The Kinks also have a new album out, *Face to Face*. The Kinks have a great sense of style and their songs are always structurally interesting. Their bag is basically ragtime, but wanders to pseudo-Eastern in "Fancy" and several other places. Other Kinks goodies include "Most Exclusive Residence for Sale", "Too Much On My Mind" and "Rainy Day in June".

We also got to hear part of the Grateful Dead album. They're very Country & Western influenced and very good also. Hope to hear more of them soon.

Great single record: "Sunday Will Never Be the Same", by Spanky & Our Gang. Really pretty.

Now for the record of the month: Get Jeff Beck's, "Hi Ho Silver Lining". Turn it over. Hidden away on the B side is something called "Beck's Bolero". Play this for an unforgettable musical experience. Play it three times in a row for best results. It will change the sound of anything you hear after it. Very strange. *<Lots of speed required.>*

Oh, wow, isn't Winter ever going to leave? We're still wearing our winter clothes and are sick of looking at ourselves. Springtime, arise! Fight back! Stomp winter now! Are you a man or a mouse?

More wahoo records:

"Pay You Back With Interest"--The Hollies
"No Easy Way Down"--The Germz
"Purple Haze"--Jimi Hendrix

We recently received a tape of records currently being played in England which have not been released here. Yes, there is a Pink Floyd! They are currently storming the charts in England with "Arnold Layne", the story of a transvestite which they have managed to do both musically and tastefully--no mean feat! Also included was a group called The Soft Machine, whose "Love Makes Sweet Music" is one of the finest records ever heard. A real mover. It's a shame that these records aren't released simultaneously in both countries.

Instead, we get junk like "Release Me" and "I Was Kaiser Bill's Batman."
UGH.

"Peace, peace, peace, peace, boogie for peace"--Woody Guthrie,
25 years ago.

"Nashville swings, but Memphis boogies."--Bill Barth

More shriek discs:

"Janey's Blues"--Janis Ian
"The Collector"--Number One
"Can't Seem to Make You Mine"--The Seeds
"Pictures of Lily"--The Who (one of the best records in history)
"Morning Glory Days"--Pleasure Fair (beautiful)
"I Blew It"--The Vacant Lot (funny)
"Without Her"--Nillson (this is one of the finest contrapuntal con-
structions I ever heard. Brilliant record.)
"Big Leg Emma"--The Mothers

The Youngbloods have recorded "Euphoria" as their latest single,
exactly four years after we started playing it. Can't keep a good song
down. Remaily could use the bread, too.

Volume VI, No. 10 (& Antonia) • July 5, 1967

This column will be mainly about the Mothers ("of Invention" was
added by an uptight record company man who obviously felt that nobody with a beard deserved the title of Mother). Anyway, we saw the
Mothers again, and are they good. Boss Mother Frank Zappa is liable
to do anything from brilliant and frenetic lead guitar to "playing" a
teenage girl, who volunteered from the audience, by tickling her so
that she screams into a microphone at appropriate intervals during a
free-form number. They're playing a lot of "serious" music now, but
still do their great old rock stuff as well.

Playing with them is someone called Uncle Meat. Continuing the policy of confusion, Uncle Meat is a girl who sings and writes her own songs. She gets a number of strange and unusual effects by using one of the best female voices ever heard in unexpected ways.

Back to the Mothers: There are eight of 'em at the moment and their musical equipment ranges through kettle drums and large Chinese gongs. They have a new album out called *Absolutely Free* which everyone should get or at least listen to. It includes their single "America Drinks and Goes Home", a true classic. They've probably never done the same set twice, as they keep coming up with new things. Their first album, *Freak Out*, is a winner also, with lots of their fantastic old rock stuff on it. Frank Zappa is one of the few people who really appreciates old rock stuff and knows how musical it is.

And what's this nonsense about putting some flowers in your hair if you go to San Francisco? That's the silliest thing since Barry McGuire.

Wow. *Sgt. Pepper's Lonely Hearts Club Band*. Wow.

Just for the record, because I haven't seen it mentioned anywhere, the Mothers can hold their own with any rock group on the planet, cut most jazz groups to ribbons, and play competently and accurately in more musical styles than anybody.

By the way, I'm cutting another record with Steve Weber. Sam Shepard will be drumming on this one, and I'm playing electrified fiddle. We really sound a lot different. We haven't recorded since 1964, and I've learned a lot of things about electricity since then. (Also my singing and rhythm are better). We should finish it the day after tomorrow, and it will be on the ESP label. It's several times better than anything we've ever done. *<Um, afraid not.>*

SON OF CREEP LIST:

Been a lot of bellyaching under the label of "soul".

"Seven Tombs of Doom"--The Four Tops
"Come to the Sunshine"--Harpers Bizarre
"The River is Wide"--The Forum
"All I Need"--The Temptations
"Up, Up and Away"--The 5th Dimension

Who couldn't fly if their bellies were bloated with helium.

Whenever I hear the phrase "flower children", I think of the Hells Angels with belladonna sprigs behind their ears. Slobs have been raving about the Bee Gees. Listen to the flip side of their record, "I Can't See Nobody". Don't he sound like Donald Duck? This is the end of the column.

<I love the Bee Gees. This was not originally intended to be the end of the column. I had just asked Antonia what else I should write, and she said, "Just write, this is the end of the column." And it turned out to be true.>